Gardening with Children

First published in 1980
by Faber and Faber Limited
3 Queen Square London WC1
Set, printed and bound in Great Britain by
Fakenham Press Limited
Fakenham Norfolk
All rights reserved

British Library Cataloguing in Publication Data

Ross, Alison
  Gardening with children
  1.   Children's gardens
  I. Title
  635   SB457

  ISBN 0–571–11564–0

GARDENING WITH CHILDREN

Alison Ross

with line drawings by Juliet Renny

FABER & FABER · London and Boston

TO JIM

Contents

Illustrations

Acknowledgements

First of all I want to acknowledge most gratefully all the help and encouragement that I have been given by the late Sir Edward Salisbury, past Director of the Royal Botanic Gardens, Kew. Then I would like to thank Mrs Peggy Betterton, ex-headmistress of St Paul's Junior School, Kingston-on-Thames, Surrey, and of Trafalgar Infant School, Twickenham, Middlesex, and Miss Elizabeth Hess, ex-principal of Studley Agricultural College for Women, for reading early drafts of my text and sharing their invaluable wisdom, educationally-speaking especially, after the years they have both spent helping children and young people to appreciate and learn about plants and gardening.

The following are only a few of those whom I should also like to thank for their readiness to add to my knowledge and to offer helpful ideas: Mrs Sally Gray, Messrs Herbert and Geoffrey Goatcher, Mrs Louise Gurrin, Mrs Marjorie Holland, Messrs Will and Paul Ingwersen, Mr David McClintock, Mr Lawrence Perkins, Mr and Mrs Bill Rynveldt and Mr Patrick Synge.

To these I must add Mr George A. McCleod of Craig House Cacti, Mr K. J. Spackman and Miss Kathleen Fleet of the Norwood Institute of Horticulture and Agriculture, Mr David Wellman of Cheals Garden Centre, Pulborough, Sussex, and, of course, the ever-gracious officials of the Disabled Living Foundation and the Gardens for the Disabled Trust.

I am grateful to Mrs Juliet Renny for all the time and trouble she has taken to make the line drawings so accurate and attractive, for the care Miss Judy Fowler took in typing my untidy drafts, and for the inexhaustible skills and tact of Miss Eileen Brooksbank, my editor at Fabers, and of Mrs Jean Robinson and for the way they have handled such a vehement author.

Finally I would like to thank my husband for all his loving and constructive patience all through my somewhat hectic work on this book.

Introduction

The value of introducing children to the delights of gardening really needs to be experienced before it can be assessed. At its simplest level, gardening is recognised as a healthy, even health-giving, and productive occupation, but the benefits that may follow if the introduction has been a happy one can be very wide-reaching indeed. During the many years I have spent gardening with children of all ages, from pre-school days onwards, I have found that it can be great fun, extremely rewarding and full of surprises. It has frequently been an illuminating experience both for them and for me and it has encouraged me to write a book to help other parents, grandparents, teachers and friends, to introduce young people to the pleasures and interests of gardening.

I have borne in mind that many adults may have little horticultural experience, and also that older children may want to use the book on their own. Knowledgeable gardeners will have no need of much of the practical advice I give, but my aim is not only to provide the basic information required by many would-be gardeners, adults and children, but also, and of equal importance, to show how children can become involved in all aspects of gardening—using that term in the widest sense. It should never be an isolated subject, especially where the young are involved, because for them it can be stimulating almost beyond belief as the diagram on p. 27 indicates.

I have written not just for those with gardens, but also for many who may have only a balcony, windowbox or backyard (possibly a schoolyard) and also for the indoor gardener, being particularly aware of the needs of housebound and handicapped young people for whom the growing of plants can be an especially absorbing activity.

Ideas are suggested for a wide range of projects, which include making ponds, building rock gardens and designing and planting miniature gardens in different types of containers, sometimes without using soil. Much space is given to ideas and advice on growing useful and decorative plants of all kinds in many different situations, but I have also been concerned to stress the variety of other interests that can be developed, paying special attention to the importance of conservation and of sharing gardens with wildlife. The extra benefits, apart from the simple visual pleasure, that can be gained from the nationally popular occupation of

garden visiting have been pointed out. Such visits can give a wider
understanding of many kinds of garden, their design and special features, and an appreciation of garden history, all of which provide topics to
be discussed later at home or in school. Continuity of interest is vital and
for this reason I suggest the making and keeping of individual Gardening
Notebooks: ideas for these are addressed to the children themselves and
are given at the end of the chapters, together with a list of subjects for
further discussion, observation and research.

Once children have been shown how to start on a particular project,
they often find they can manage on their own and they begin to plan and
investigate for themselves. Caring for plants will give them a special
interest and a sense of responsibility, and in my first chapter I have
indicated some of the ways in which, from simple beginnings, such
activities can be extended and their lives enriched.

Glossary

AERATE To introduce air.

ALPINE A plant that grows in high mountainous regions.

AMPHIBIAN A creature which lives on land and at times in water.

ANNUAL A plant that grows, flowers and seeds all in one year.

ANTHER The part of the stamen of the flower that bears pollen (see Fig. 2).

AQUATIC A plant that grows in, or very close to, water.

ARBORETUM A special garden containing a collection of trees (plural—arboreta).

AREOLE A tuft of short hairs or fluffy wool out of which cactus spines grow.

AROMATIC Fragrant, or spicy smelling.

BACTERIA Tiny living bodies, invisible to the naked eye, some of which are useful in the soil, especially in rotting down plant and animal materials to make humus and compost.

BEDDING-OUT PLANTS Young plants, usually annuals or biennials, which can be bought from nurseries and garden centres ready to be planted out into the places where they are to flower.

BIENNIAL A plant that takes two years to flower and seed, and then dies.

BIODEGRADABLE Made from materials which will rot down.

BROWSE To feed, as grazing animals do, on plants or young, low-growing tree twigs and branches, thus making a neat 'browse line'.

CACTUS A plant with thick and often fleshy swollen stems capable of growing in very dry conditions.

CARBOY A large, globe-shaped glass bottle used to hold liquids.

CARPEL The seed-holding, female organ of a flower (see Fig. 2).

CHLOROPHYLL The green colouring-matter in plants which enables them to manufacture food.

COMPOST: GARDEN Garden and kitchen waste materials rotted down to produce a useful soil-improving fertiliser.

COMPOST HEAP The heap of such waste materials used to make garden compost.

COMPOST: GROWING Specially prepared soil (commercially available), usually based on peat, with sand, soil nutrients, and sometimes loam added, which is used for growing plants in pots and containers.

COMPOST: SEED-SOWING As above, prepared specifically for seed sowing and for rooting cuttings.

CONIFER A cone-bearing tree.

CONSERVATION Looking after the environment for the benefit of all who use it, including, of course, the plants and animals.

CORM A bulb-like swollen base of a stem.

COTYLEDONS The first leaves produced by the seed when it germinates. They are present in the seed and often contain food reserves for the plant's initial sustenance.

CROCKS Broken bits of earthenware and other pots used to cover the bottom and drainage holes of flower pots and other growing containers.

CULTIVAR A cultivated variety produced when nurserymen actually pollinate one species with pollen from another or select out a particular plant with special characteristics.

CUTTING A small piece of stem, leaf or root taken from a growing plant, which is encouraged to produce roots and form a new plant.

DECIDUOUS A tree that sheds, and later renews, its leaves annually.

DESICCANT A substance which withdraws and holds moisture.

DROUGHT A long period of dry weather, causing lack of moisture in the soil.

EMBRYO A tiny immature plant still in the seed.

ENTOMOLOGIST Someone who studies insects.

EVAPORATION The loss of moisture from solids or liquids in the form of water vapour.

EVERGREEN A tree that bears leaves all the year round.

EXOTIC A plant that has been introduced from abroad.

FASTIGIATE A tree with branches which grow almost erect, giving it a thin narrow shape.

FERTILISATION The joining of the contents of the pollen grain with that of the female egg cell so that a fertile seed can develop.

FERTILISER The nutrient-rich materials added to the soil to provide food for the plants.

FILAMENT The stalk of a stamen (see Fig. 2).

FLOATER A water plant with floating leaves, and sometimes flowers, but with unanchored roots.

FLORET One of the small flowers which together make up a flower head or inflorescence.

FOLLY An apparently useless building, often in a fancy style, built in the past as a decoration in large gardens.

FROND The leaf-like growth of ferns.

FRUIT   The total remains of one flower which hold the ripe seed or seeds.

GAZEBO   A building, or structure of some kind, sometimes on a hill, from which a view can be obtained.

GENUS   A division of a plant family based on the plant's botanical characteristics and used to indicate its first botanical name (plural—genera).

GERMINATION   The beginning of a seed's development, when it puts out young roots and shoots.

GROTTO   An artificial ornamental tunnel, cave or shell house.

HA-HA   A sunken, and usually empty, dyke or ditch, used in gardens constructed in the past to keep out grazing animals in place of a wall, fence or hedge and so give an uninterrupted view from the house.

HERBACEOUS   A perennial flowering plant.

HERBACEOUS BORDER   A flower border containing herbaceous plants.

HERBICIDE   A chemical weed-killer, frequently poisonous.

HUMUS   The decayed remains of plant material in the soil.

HYBRID   A new plant which is the offspring of two different species of plants. This is usually indicated by an × between their two botanical names.

IMMORTELLE   An everlasting flower.

INORGANIC   Composed of man-made materials.

INSECTICIDE   A chemical insect-killer, frequently poisonous.

KNOT GARDEN   A garden, common in Elizabethan times, which was laid out in complicated patterns of small, low beds often surrounded by short, clipped hedges.

LAYER   A shoot from a parent plant, which sends out roots and can then be detached to form a separate plant.

LOAM   Soil composed of a balanced mixture of sand, clay and humus.

MARGINAL WATER PLANT   A plant growing at the edge of a pool or stream.

MAZE   A complicated layout of hedged paths forming a puzzle walk.

MULCH   A soft layer of compost, other plant material or dung put on top of the soil to conserve moisture and prevent weed growth.

NECTAR   Sweet plant juices produced by plants, which bees collect and convert to honey, and other insects also use for direct food.

NODE   The point where one or more leaves grow from the stem.

NUTRIENTS   Substances that provide plant nourishment, including elements such as nitrogen, phosphorus, iron, potassium and magnesium.

OFFSETS   New young shoots from main stem or roots, including new bulbs, which are produced on the sides of some bulbous plants.

ORGANIC   Composed of natural, rather than man-made materials.

ORGANISM   A living plant or animal body.

OXYGENATING PLANTS   Those grown in water, keeping it fresh by giving off oxygen.

PARASITE   A plant that grows in, or on, another plant and obtains nourishment from it.

PARTERRE   A wide, level area in a garden, often laid out with complicated patterns of flower beds, some of which may be filled with very low-growing plants to make patterned carpet beds.

PENDULOUS   Drooping or hanging down.

PERENNIAL   A plant that goes on living, flowering and seeding for several years.

PERIANTH   The sepals and petals of a flower together (see Fig. 2).

PESTICIDE   A substance, frequently poisonous, for destroying pests.

PETALS   The inner 'flower leaves' which are often brightly coloured to attract insects to the flowers (see Fig. 2).

pH   A term used to rate the acidity or alkalinity of the soil.

PHOTOSYNTHESIS   The process of the manufacture of food by the green parts of the plant using air, light and water.

POLLEN   The male cells of plants, the contents of which fertilise the female egg cells.

POLLINATION:
  CROSS-POLLINATION   The taking of pollen from the male part of one flower to the female part of another by insects, wind or other methods.
  SELF-POLLINATION   The fertilisation of the female part of the flower by pollen from the male part of the same flower.

POROUS   Having minute holes which permit air and liquids to pass through them.

PROPAGATION   The growing of new plants either from seeds or vegetatively from parts of existing ones.

PROSTRATE   Lying or growing very close to the ground.

PRUNING   Cutting away or trimming back dead, unwanted or overgrown branches or twigs of trees and shrubs.

ROOTSTOCK   The roots and main stem of an established plant, in which the scion or bud is inserted for propagation.

ROSETTE   A circular ground-hugging arrangement of leaves that protects the plant's ground space.

SCION   A shoot of a plant cut for grafting.

SEED   The product of one fertilised egg cell of a plant.

SEEDLING   A young plant raised from seed.

SEPALS   The outer 'flower leaves' which are frequently green and can act as bud coverings (see Fig. 2).

Glossary

SHRUB A woody plant, usually shorter than a tree even when fully grown, with several woody stems near the ground rather than one woody stem or trunk.

SPECIES A sub-division of a genus, used to designate a particular plant or animal (abbreviated to sp in the singular and spp in the plural).

SPORE The reproductive product of some non-flowering plants such as ferns.

STAMENS The male organs of the flower (see Fig. 2).

STERILISATION The treatment of a substance, often by heat, so that it contains no living organisms.

STIGMA The sticky, pollen-catching disc or head of the carpel that receives the pollen (see Fig. 2).

STOLON A runner or long, low creeping stem (see Fig. 2).

STYLE The stalk holding the stigma and connecting it to the carpel (see Fig. 2).

SUBSOIL The layer of the earth directly under the soil.

SUCCULENT A plant that usually grows naturally in very dry conditions and is able to store moisture in its thick fleshy leaves, stems and branches for use in periods of drought.

TENDER PLANTS Those which grow in warm conditions and are easily killed by frost or very cold weather.

TENDRIL A slender, clinging plant organ, sensitive enough to twine around anything with which it comes in contact.

TILTH Usually the top layer of fine, well-cultivated soil.

TISANE A herbal infusion, similar to tea, made by pouring boiling water over herbs which are often fragrant and spicy. Many tisanes have healthful properties.

TOPIARY The art of clipping trees and shrubs into ornamental shapes.

TOXIC Poisonous.

TRANSPIRATION The giving off of water vapour by plants.

TRANSPLANT To move and replant from one place to another.

TUBER A thick, swollen underground plant stem which stores food.

TUFA ROCK A light, porous rock that is quarried in places rich in certain special mineral springs.

TURGID Leaves which are swollen and firm rather than wilting through lack of moisture.

VARIEGATED A leaf which is marked by regular or irregular stripes and patches of white, cream or yellow.

VARIETY A naturally produced rather than a cultivated form of a plant.

VIVIPAROUS A plant that produces tiny, young plants on its leaves or stems while they are still growing and attached to the main plant.

WATERLOGGED Completely saturated with water.

1 · Sharing the pleasure of gardening

When introducing children to gardening it soon becomes obvious that beginners fall into three major categories. The first are those young gardeners who seem to have been born with gardening intuition and a love of the soil and all living things. They handle plants with great sensitivity and everything grows for them—they are, as we say, 'green-fingered'.

Then there is a far bigger group of children who are full of latent interest that is ready to burst into life. They only need triggering off with encouragement and few demonstrations before they are away, happily employed in all kinds of work and schemes. The work has probably been thought out or even prepared in advance by the adult, but this type of child will be full of ideas for exploring the project more deeply and will only need subsequent guidance. This group includes those who delight in, for example, looking out for flowers, 'seed-boxes' and the seeds which develop in them; they are quick to notice insects that alight on the flowers and to comment on birds and other living creatures that they see.

It is the children in the third group who provide the biggest challenge. They need an interesting introduction, one that has been carefully thought out, to catch their attention. They may be slower and need far more help and it is important that their individual preferences should be pursued once an attendant adult has had a glimpe of them. They are less easy to involve in individual schemes, but often work better with others, and it is fascinating to watch their interests beginning to expand. Curiously enough, these are the children who will, in many cases, prove to be the most dedicated, although they may, especially in the early stages, be the most demanding.

Most children enjoy watching adults, asking questions and learning that way. All enquiries along the lines of 'What are you doing?' 'What are you doing it for?' and 'Why are you doing it that way?' need answering sensibly and with patience. If a few explanatory comments prove to interest the watchers, the adult who is in the garden has to be prepared to abandon his own pursuit of the moment to devote his whole attention to the child. Sometimes an admirable introduction to the joys of gardening is started off in this way and it could be the time to start looking at different

kinds of gardens, garden centres, museums and nurseries. It all depends
on the age of the children and, of course, on their backgrounds and the
conditions in which they will be able to proceed with their own gardening
activities.

It may often prove interesting to adults to see how the various aspects
of gardening attract and appeal to different children. Some show delight
in using miniature equipment and plants; others seem to need heavier
work and revel in building walls, making bonfires, digging holes for
ponds, laying paths or helping with the erection of sheds. These contrasting outlooks cannot be divided into chosen tasks for girls and boys, as
many little girls delight in wielding a hammer or struggling with recalci-
trant sheets of polythene while some of the toughest boys seem to derive
much satisfaction from pricking out and planting delicate seedlings.

As in all things, the adults have to be very perceptive: their age is
unimportant for they can act as excellent gardening companions to children at all stages of their lives. All they need to have initially is a little
plant-growing experience and an enormous amount of patience, com-
bined with a love of learning. Clearly they must be fond of children and
enjoy being with them, but they can range in age from older teenagers
and students, including student nurses, to retired teachers and grandparents who often make first-rate guides. They need not have a garden,
for there are plenty of indoor gardening pursuits that children will enjoy
undertaking and benefit from finding out about.

Gardening *with* children, perhaps it should be made clear now, does
not necessarily mean working with them every minute of the time, nor
having to work together, shoulder to shoulder, although occasions may
arise when an adult's abilities and strength can be helpful. Generally
speaking, though, it means being within reach and available always with
help, suggestions and answers to questions when they are needed.

It also means being prepared to admit personal ignorance. 'I don't
know. Let's look it up' is a far better answer than a faltering, possibly
nonsensical reply, and indeed, anyone who is involved with gardening
and children should have a joy in the sense of discovery as well as some
knowledge of where to start finding the answers. It is always interesting
to have to look things up, and the pursuing of enquiries can be shared and
everyone's knowledge increased. The booklist and the list of some useful
addresses at the back of this book will act as a guide. Children should be
encouraged to make full use of the glossary and indexes provided: in any
book of this kind it is necessary for particular topics to be discussed in
more than one chapter, and although the cross references in the text will
be a help, the value of the indexes should be stressed.

As regards practical work, there are a couple of pitfalls for the guiding adult to avoid. One is the ill-founded idea that children always like helping adults. They often don't. They only like helping when they want to, are particularly interested or suggest it themselves. They are not philanthropists, so even if they have once 'helped' in a garden, they must never be counted on for future occasions. Their offer must be entirely voluntary which means that it must be engendered in a subtler way than by asking for it. But sharing interests is quite a different matter and most children enjoy researching with adults.

The other pitfall is to offer a child its own garden, possibly within the parents' or grandparents' garden, or at school, before it is ready for it. It is wiser to wait until some indication is made that an individual patch would be appreciated and then to allocate, after consultation together, a good rather than scruffy place.

Children's interest can easily be lost and it is essential to be ready with endless encouragement and ideas, so as to provide a continuation of activities. At the end of each of the following chapters is a section addressed to the children themselves and this contains suggestions for the keeping of *Gardening Notebooks* and for *Further Topics for Discussion, Observation and Research* (for the first example, see p. 37). The ideas given are only starters and will be added to by the adults and by the children themselves as various lines of interest show. Many of them could lead to group or class activities. The notebooks should belong to individual children and be used for their personal records and comments. They can be begun when children are very young and able to make pictures or montages from coloured flower-picture cut-outs and scraps, and then the records should start, in a small way at first, once the children are able to write. The notebooks should be loose-leaf, large and sturdy and children can cover them in strong plastic material which can be imaginatively decorated. They may start neat and flat but will grow as leaflets and cuttings are collected, and they should include both lined and unlined paper for writing and drawing. Descriptions of all gardening activities and impressions from expeditions to see other gardens should be written so that the children will feel that keeping and improving their notebooks is part of their gardening programme. Catching up with records, adding extra information, choosing, pasting in and drawing pictures make valuable occupations on days when the weather is too bad, or the child not fit enough, to carry on with practical tasks outside. Some of the 'Further Topics' outlined may involve visits to public libraries, and these can be reserved for weekends and holiday times—though good school libraries will probably contain some of the books needed for research.

Adults should encourage children to write, as well as to talk, about their pleasure in, or dislike of, various aspects of gardening and wildlife, and also to create verse which need not rhyme. It is helpful to both articulate and inarticulate children to have experience in this type of writing and it also helps to improve their observation.

A hand lens of a X8 or X10 magnification is a small piece of equipment which adds greatly to every gardener's interest and knowledge. These often prove to be of tremendous interest to children and it can be an adult's privilege to provoke and encourage the use of such a magnifying glass. Some children find them easier to use than others; some even carry them with them all the time on a string round their necks, as many adult field naturalists do, and are always stopping to peer at flowers, leaves, roots, dead insects' wings or legs, and discarded birds' feathers.

A maximum/minimum thermometer is another tool that can add interest to both indoor and outdoor gardening and the regular reading should be included in the Gardening Notebook, together with comments on prevalent weather conditions.

It is necessary for all gardeners, young and older, to learn the scientific, botanical or Latinised plant names and to use them constantly. They are not hard to learn and children have no difficulty whatsoever in picking them up, as they trip off their tongues with a facility which is enviable to many adults. It may appear to be too academic a point to stress, but it is truly essential now because these names are in universal use, and it does avoid real confusion. 'Blue bonnets' may be a charming and simple name for, say, monkshood (*Aconitum napellus*) (**P**)[1], but it is frequently also used in different localities, even in this country, for at least five or six other plants, including cornflower (*Centaurea cyanus*), columbine (*Aquilegia vulgaris*) and bluebell (*Endymion non-scriptus*), so that its definitive qualities are non-existent. The naming of plants is explained on p. 73.

The chapters which follow each collate material to aid the guiding adult in starting and helping with various projects or short spells of work in different types of gardening activity. They aim to give suggestions for work, together with a basic amount of biological and horticultural information as a background. This is so that any adults who are not particularly up-to-date or knowledgeable themselves will be in a better position after reading them to answer some of the inevitable questions which will be asked and then to go ahead without any serious hold-ups. Ideas are given so that teachers, parents, grandparents and others are confident enough to begin gardening with children and carrying out different schemes; something they may have thought of doing but not yet started.

Gardening as such, the planting and tending of seedlings and grown

---

[1] (**P**) is the symbol used in the index to indicate that a plant is poisonous. A list of such plants is given in Appendix 2.

plants, obviously forms the hub of the wheel and becomes the centre of endless 'spokes'. It can be quite fun for a child and an adult to sit down together and draw a chart of possible raying-out extensions and probably far more fun for several children, or a class, to get together and each make their own, deciding which of them would like to follow up which ray. The diagram below showing possible extensions of activities was made by children of 11. It is included as an example to show that there is never any need to worry that there may not be enough to do. In fact it is more a question of being selective about choosing the extensions so that they will prove to be of maximum interest. The possibilities are virtually limitless and the benefits may be unending.

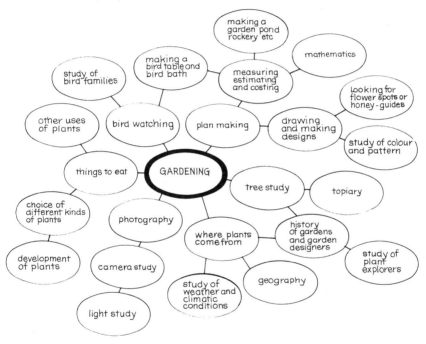

1. Extensions of interest arising from gardening

2 · Wildlife in the garden

All gardens, small or large, whether they are in towns, suburbs or rural areas, can become far more interesting and valuable places if their owners are happy to share them with wildlife.

Indeed most country-lovers, naturalists and conservationists realise how urgent it is, now that so much land is being used for building and road-making, to try to help various forms of wildlife to continue to survive. Places where they used to be safe are disappearing fast, so it now seems that the least we can do is to offer them the safe hospitality of our gardens.

Gardens make excellent nature reserves where different sections of the extremely complicated web of life can be observed. Any child with keen eyesight or a sharp ear is capable of helping research into the habits of wildlife and this can easily be done in a garden. It might be helpful to make enquiries at the local public library for the name of the secretary of the nearest natural history society, or even specialist naturalists who live nearby. Such groups or individuals are usually interested to do all they can to encourage children's enthusiasm and to offer suggestions for simple research projects that could be undertaken. There are also some books on wildlife in the garden which will help here (see p. 36).

Our positive attitude of being prepared to share our gardens with wild creatures will be repaid over and over again. However, no wildlife finds much of a welcome and few creatures stay long, even if they ever visit, in overneat gardens which have beds of regimented flowers with lack of shelter in between, weedless paths and well-manicured lawns. Instead they prefer areas where plants grow close together, providing them with plenty of cover so that they can eat undisturbed. Insects, too, prefer a garden with an infinite variety of flowering plants for them to visit.

Bees and hedgehogs are frequently said to be two of the gardener's best friends, but many forms of animal life can be an actual asset to the garden. Below is a list of creatures for children to look out for. Their help far exceeds any damage they may do.

NAME OF CREATURE	USEFULNESS IN THE GARDEN
Earthworms	Help to break up and also to aerate the soil. Carry dead leaves and other humus down into the soil.

NAME OF CREATURE	USEFULNESS IN THE GARDEN
Spiders	Catch and kill undesirable flies and other insects. Some hunting spiders also suck and kill wood-lice.
Harvestmen	Eat green-flies and other aphids.

Insects

Honey-bees, bumblebees and solitary bees	All of great importance to man because they carry pollen, on their heads and bodies, from flower to flower, thus bringing about pollination and starting off the process of seed and fruit development.
Long-tongued moths and some flies, including hover-flies	Help in pollination.
Ladybirds, lacewing flies and a few hover-fly larvae	Eat green-flies and black-flies.

Resident birds

Blackbirds	Eat numerous pests, including the grubs, or larvae, of craneflies (daddy-long-legs), called leatherjackets, slugs and small snails.
Song thrushes	Eat more or less the same pests as blackbirds, plus many small snails, especially in dry weather.
Robins	Eat a wide variety of tiny harmful pests as well as wireworms and millipedes.
Wrens	Eat many small pests, including mosquitoes, gnats and aphids.
Blue tits, great tits, coal tits and marsh tits	Eat much the same pests as wrens. Blue tits take more aphids off the leaves of growing plants and great tits also eat the caterpillars, or larvae, of leaf-eating moths. Coal tits and marsh tits tend to work more on pests on tree bark.
Dunnocks or hedge sparrows	Eat many small insects, including the larvae of some moths, and also an assortment of weed seeds.
Chaffinches, greenfinches and goldfinches	Eat many weed seeds, including those of groundsel, dandelion, daisy and thistle.

Summer migrants

Chiffchaffs, willow warblers, blackcaps and common whitethroats	Eat a great number of tiny insects and other invertebrate pests, particularly the larvae of destructive moths and some aphids.
Cuckoos	Eat caterpillars, even those with hairy bodies.
Swallow, swifts and house martins	Eat many insects in the air over gardens, building their nests on houses and sheds or, in the case of the first two, on rafters inside.

NAME OF CREATURE   USEFULNESS IN THE GARDEN
Reptiles and amphibians
Common lizards,   Eat slugs and a variety of other pests including
slow-worms, common   leatherjackets.
frogs, toads and newts

Mammals
Hedgehogs   Eat many slugs, snails and other plant-destroying pests.

POLLINATION

The reproductive organs of flowering plants are in the flowers themselves, often right in the centre, and it is the flowers that act as advertising
hoardings to attract visits from honey and bumblebees, wasps, hover-
flies and other insects. In most plants seed can only be set if the pollen
from the anthers of one flower is carried by these insects to the female
organs of another. This is known as cross-pollination. It is the first stage of
the fertilisation process which is completed when the pollengrain contents reach, penetrate and fuse with the female egg cell, or ovum, so that
the seed can then start developing. (Some plants with flowers of both
sexes can pollinate themselves, and are said to be self-pollinating.) The
remaining part of the flower consists of the perianth leaves of which the
outer ring are known as the sepals, which are usually greenish and vary
greatly in thickness and texture. They fold back, or fall off, as the petals
begin to expand and show. The inner ring, the petals, can be coloured,
sometimes green or white, and attract insects to the flower. They are
sometimes converted into nectar-holding or -producing organs or they
may just develop basal pouches for this purpose.

The male organs of the flower are the stamens which consist of a
pollen-containing head or anther, which is usually held up by a stalk or
filament. The female organs, known collectively as the ovaries, are made
up from carpels which contain egg cells, or ova (singular—ovum). Each
carpel is topped by a sticky, pollen-catching disc, the stigma, which is
often held aloft on a stalk, or style. All these parts of the flower, including
the sepals and petals, are attached to the receptacle which is the holder or
base of the flower. The majority of flowering plants have male and female
organs in the *same* flower, but there are some which have these organs in
separate flowers. Hazel trees are an example of this: their long yellow
catkins hold the male pollen-bearing parts, while small buds hold the
female organs and produce thin, red tufts (the stigmas), at their tips all
ready to catch the windblown pollen. These will eventually bear the
fruit—nuts in this case (see page 88 for a 'further topic' on catkins).

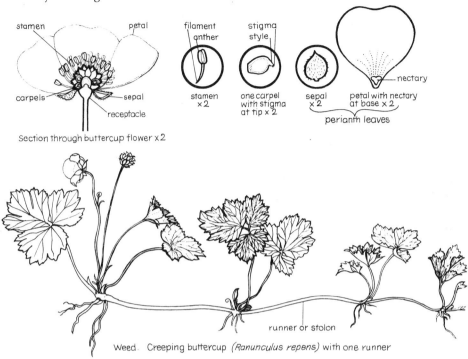

Section through buttercup flower x2

Weed. Creeping buttercup *(Ranunculus repens)* with one runner

2. *The parts of a flower*

HOW TO ENCOURAGE WILDLIFE INTO THE GARDEN

Hive, or honey, bees, the valuable bumblebees and other pollinating insects are primarily attracted into the garden by scented flowers. The hive, or honey, bees are those that are now kept by beekeepers in hives, while the bumblebees, large and furry-bodied, are wild and often form their colonies underground. Bees can see flowers in shades of crimson, blue and purple better than those of other colours although they do visit and alight on many other single blossoms. Double flowers have an increased number of petals which have taken the place of pollen-producing anthers and nectaries (the nectar containers) so these do not attract the useful pollinating insects.

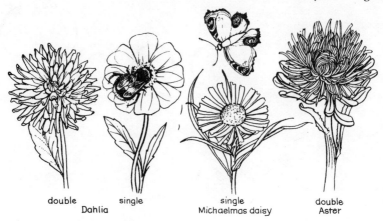

double   single   single   double
Dahlia   Michaelmas daisy   Aster

3. Two double and two single flowers

Here is a list of a few of the herbaceous plants, shrubs and trees that are useful to attract bees into the garden (the botanical naming of plants is discussed in chapter 4):

Apple (*Malus domestica*); aubrieta (*Aubrieta deltoidea*); baby blue eyes (*Nemophila menziesii*); blackberry (*Rubus fruticosus*); butterfly bush (*Buddleia davidii*); catmint (*Nepeta×faassenii*); single cherries (*Prunus* spp); crab apples (*Malus* spp); crocuses (*Crocus* spp); elder (*Sambucus nigra*); fishbone cotoneaster (*Cotoneaster horizontalis*); foxgloves (*Digitalis* spp); heathers (*Calluna vulgaris* cultivars); hollies (*Ilex* spp and cultivars) particularly the female types; honesty (*Lunaria annua*); honeysuckles (*Lonicera* spp); horse chestnut (*Aesculus hippocastanum*); ice plant (*Sedum spectabile*); ivies (*Hedera* spp) left to flower; lavender (*Lavandula spica*); limes (*Tilia* spp) except silver-leaved ones; Michaelmas daisy (*Aster novi-belgii*); pears (*Pyrus* spp); plum (*Prunus domestica*); poached egg plant (*Limnanthes douglasii*); polyanthus (*Primula* hybrids and cultivars); privet (*Ligustrum ovalifolium*) left to flower; raspberry (*Rubus idaeus*); red valerian (*Kentranthus ruber*); single roses (*Rosa* spp); rosemary (*Rosmarinus officinalis*); rowan (*Sorbus aucuparia*); sweet chestnut (*Castanea sativa*); thymes (*Thymus* app); wallflowers (*Cheiranthus* spp); willows (*Salix* spp).

More-comprehensive lists and valuable information about bees in the garden can be obtained by sending 35p (for handling charges) to the International Bee Research Association (see p. 166).

Butterflies may help a little in pollination but, more than anything, they are creatures that give sheer delight in summer gardens. There are several different kinds which visit gardens, many with showy markings on their wings which make their identification from a butterfly book relatively simple for children. As so many of the butterflies' favourite plants are being destroyed in the countryside, gardeners can do a great deal to help conserve them and give them a chance to breed and survive.

Butterflies visit an enormous number of single flowers in search of nectar. Like bees, their visual range seems best between the crimson-reds, mauves, purples and purplish-blues, although they also go to some white and yellow flowers. It seems that many of the plants with these coloured flowers have scented blooms and the presence of scent is usually a sign that the flower also produces nectar.

They also need what are known, rather ambiguously, as their food plants, on which the adult butterflies lay their eggs, so that succeeding generations of caterpillars (larvae) may hatch, then go into pupation (the chrysalis form) and eventually emerge as new adults.

As both bees and butterflies need the sweet plant juices, or nectar, from flowers, many of their favourite flowers are the same. The list of plants which will attract bees into the garden, on p. 32, is therefore also a guide to those which will encourage butterflies. Some of these are also special butterfly food plants—orange tip butterflies lay their eggs on honesty; in gardens, holly blues use both ivy and female holly and white admirals lay on honeysuckle. But some species, the red admirals, peacocks, small tortoiseshells and commas, just need healthy nettle plants for their eggs and the developing caterpillars and pupae.

As can be seen from the list of creatures on p. 29, some birds can be a great help to gardeners. They are most interesting to watch and they eat many small insects and other normally harmful creatures as well as weed seeds. But, if they are to make their homes nearby, they need trees or thick shrubs, including some that produce berries for food, that they can use for perching, for songposts and for roosting in at night. They need secluded areas and places where they can collect nesting materials, so that they can build nests and raise their families in peace.

Birds can usually be encouraged into the garden by providing a bird table for food in bad weather and a pan of fresh drinking and bathing water all the year round, both of which must be kept out of reach of marauding cats. Flat-dwellers can place them on windowsills so that they too can enjoy the wildlife of the locality.

It is important that children feed the birds only when they need extra food to supplement their normal diets. That is, of course, in the winter in hard weather and, sometimes, in early spring and late autumn, if the ground is parched. Wild birds should not be fed while they are feeding their young as much of the food that is suitable for adults is not suitable for nestlings and may well kill them. There are many records of nestfuls of blue tits and great tits that have been choked to death by lumps of fat and whole peanuts that their parents have brought to them straight from the bird table.

Only fresh food should be used when feeding birds and any that is stale should be removed from the garden before it goes rancid. The food should be cut or minced up so that the birds can get hold of it easily in their beaks. Any foods that contain chocolate, or those that are heavily salted, such as bacon, are poisonous to birds. Apart from placing it on a bird table which is safe from cats, the food can be put in many different containers, such as fine-meshed nets, special nut holders and other types of hanging, wire-framed nets.

The Royal Society for the Protection of Birds (see p. 167) offers some interesting free literature about making gardens attractive to birds, as well as information about food and feeding apparatus, bird baths and nesting boxes. This is all available on receipt of a large, stamped, self-addressed envelope. There is a flourishing junior section and they also sell recordings of bird song, which are useful for beginners.

Sadly, the fact must be faced that there are some birds that are not particularly welcome in gardens, especially those like wood pigeons, collared doves and bullfinches (even though beautiful) which can cause destruction to gardeners' precious plants. Therefore they have to be discouraged and it is interesting for children to think of harmless ways of keeping them away. All kinds of glittering, brightly coloured mobiles can be made from tin foil and plastics and strung up

a Robin
b Song thrush
c Greater spotted woodpecker
d Blue tits

4. A bird table

5. *Some bird scarers*

a Scarecrow with stick
b Line of coloured plastic pennants
c Glittering and jingling milk bottle tops
d Aluminium foil small windmills

over the growing plants. Scarecrows can be fun to make too. Curiously enough, the resident garden birds seem to take little notice of these scarers and robins, wrens and even blue tits have actually been known to nest in scarecrows.

Although toads, frogs and newts are mentioned in the list of helpful wildlife, they are unlikely to stay in gardens unless they have available permanent ponds or pools in which to breed. Suggestions for making a pond are given in Chapter 8. If there is a pond in the garden (especially if it is not stocked with greedy fish) the child will be able to watch the interesting aquatic stages in the life cycles of these amphibians, as well as of smaller creatures, such as dragonflies, damselflies, water boatmen, water beetles, water spiders, water scorpions, caddis flies and water fleas.

Finally, all gardens benefit from the presence of hedgehogs which demolish quantities of slugs, snails and other harmful pests. If they are to become resident they need rough corners from which they can collect and pile up big mounds of dead leaves and grass. These are their nests and they use them to sleep in during the daytime and eventually, if they find a mate, to breed in. If a saucerful of bread and milk is put out for them each day at dusk in the same place, they quickly become tame and are a joy to watch.

This is by no means always the happy end to the story of sharing a garden with wild creatures for, while providing places where they can find food, privacy, shelter and building materials, it is useless to think of encouraging them into a garden if poisonous insect pest-killers (pesticides or insecticides) or weed-killers (herbicides) are ever used.

Where children are involved in gardening activities adults will, in any case, understand how dangerous it would be to have poisonous substances about, for the risks involved are well known. What may not be fully realised is that many of such toxic materials, whether in the form of sprays, powders or solid pellets, can do great harm in the garden. Their effects are wide reaching for they do not stop at killing unwanted creatures or weeds but can also injure and kill the wildlife that would ordinarily feed on just the creatures that the poisons have been prepared to destroy.

It looks, therefore, like a personal choice: either give up the use of poisonous pesticides, insecticides and herbicides or give up the idea of inviting wildlife into the garden. An increasing number of people now *want* to make their gardens into small nature reserves but feel they must be sure that resident or visiting mammals, birds and other small creatures are perfectly safe there. But what can be done if some pests become too much for their natural enemies to cope with and weeds seem uncontrollable?

Much research into this and other gardening problems is now being done and one of the first things that gardeners can do is to write to the Henry Doubleday Research Association (HDRA), whose address is on p. 166, asking for details of membership and for their booklist (see also the titles given on p. 163), together with any free information they can supply. A large stamped self-addressed envelope should be enclosed with any requests of this kind.

This Association's informative booklets advise gardeners on the control of pests without the use of poisonous chemicals and give examples of the ways in which various carnivorous creatures prey upon and eat others—for example, ladybirds demolish green-flies and some species of hover-fly larvae get rid of black-flies. Biological control, or control of pests by their own natural enemies, is a most interesting subject and there is need for much more careful observation to add further information to scientists' existing knowledge.

GARDENING NOTEBOOK

1. Start a dated list of all the wild creatures seen in the garden. If you do not have a garden, look out for creatures in a park or common that you visit regularly. Rule columns in your notebook so that you can record the name of the creature, where it was when seen (including the name of the plant, if it was on one), and the weather at the time. Do the creatures you see visit the garden or park regularly or are their visits haphazard?
2. On a whole page, or two facing pages, plan out a picture of a bird table (see Fig. 4) and its surroundings in a garden and stick on, or trace and colour, pictures of birds as they come into the garden. Some birds may only be seen flying over the garden so leave plenty of room for the sky in the picture.
3. Make a note of any birds that you see collecting nesting materials. Record their names, the date and what they were using to build their nests. Never disturb nesting birds but try to watch their activities, through binoculars if a pair can be borrowed.
4. Use a good insect book (see p. 161) to help identification of the various groups of insects that visit gardens.
5. Arrange a visit to a beekeeper's hives. Make notes on what you see and find out if there are any demonstration, glass-sided hives in your neighbourhood where the bees can actually be watched while they work.
6. Look out, particularly carefully, for different kinds of bumblebees. There are about eight common species which visit gardens. Notice their furry, different-coloured coats and the fact that the big queens may vary in size from over 2·5 cm, or an inch, to approximately half this size. The worker bumblebees, which are about in summer, are much smaller. Make careful notes on any you watch and try to add the names of the flowers which they visit.

FURTHER TOPICS FOR DISCUSSION, OBSERVATION AND RESEARCH

1. Collect any discarded bird feathers you find. Read descriptions of feathers (see p. 161) and try to find out where those you find have come from. Notice that the shape of the flight feathers and the tail feathers, for example, vary. Look carefully at the web of the feathers through a lens and see how light but pliable and strong they are.

2. Try to find out some of the old descriptive nouns for a group of birds, like a charm of goldfinches or a lilt of linnets.

3. Look out for pictures of the butterflies you see. Never try to catch any, but take a butterfly book (see p. 161) out to the garden and compare the butterflies with the illustrations to find out if the wings of the various species that visit your flowers show whether they are male or female.

4. At the beginning of the last century very young children were employed as bird scarers. Find out more about this and the development of scarecrows.

5. Discuss your feelings, and listen to other people's ideas, about sharing your garden with wildlife. Also discuss the need to take care of the environment and the remaining riches of the earth.

3 · Making a start—soil and tools

Soil is important to growing plants because it gives firm anchorage for their roots and provides nutrients which the young hairs on these roots can absorb. Trace elements of such vital plant foods as nitrogen, calcium, phosphorus, potassium and iron are taken in with the moisture from the humus.

Soil consists of the broken-up top layer of the earth's rocky crust together with humus, the decayed remains of natural plant and animal materials. The soil usually covers the subsoil which has little or no humus in it and lies in varying depths, according to its situation and the type of rock beneath it. Throughout the country, and even within a fairly small locality, soils can vary greatly in appearance, according to their under-lying rock types. Colours vary from dark to pale brown or even brick-red and textures may be sticky, well broken up or dry and loose. Some soils contain many large or small pebbles while others have very few.

As the make-up of soil depends on the rocks from which it came, so do the proportions of its various constituents. Some of the differences in various soils can be seen by children if they collect samples of soils from a range of different places, such as a chalky area, a leafy woodland floor and a heavy clay path. Taking a sample from their own garden will enable children to find out more about the soil's characteristics. Samples should be transported home in separate polythene bags and then placed in clean, lidded glass jars or clear polythene, flat-bottomed, corkable tubes. Each container should be carefully labelled with the place where the soil was found, then filled almost to the top with water and the top sealed with the lid or cork. They should be shaken gently but firmly so that the contents are well mixed up, and left to stand for a few hours.

As the soils begin to settle, the children will be able to see the layers. These will be of different thicknesses in each container but usually, once they have had long enough to settle completely, there will be four distinct layers. These are, from the top:

1. Humus, some of which will be floating on top of the water.
2. Very fine particles of silt and clay.
3. Coarser particles, including sand.
4. The coarsest particles and pebbles.

THE HUMUS is an important part of the soil because it helps to hold moisture and contains the soil nutrients. It also includes the very small organisms, particularly the bacteria, which are of great use in helping natural materials to decay, even though they are invisible to the naked eye. Most garden soils need to have more humus added to them and this can be done in several ways:

a) By digging-in broken-up damp peat which is clean and light to handle. Peat is old, partially-fossilised vegetable matter, often the remains of mosses or sedges, which has been compressed for centuries. It is a valuable asset to gardeners and can be used as a mulch and in composts (see pp. 43 and 44).

b) By adding well-rotted leaf-mould which may be bought, collected carefully in small quantities from woodlands or made at home, by leaving special heaps of swept-up leaves to rot down.

c) By using home-made compost (see Appendix 1).

d) By using well-rotted, not fresh, animal dung or manure.

THE FINE SILT AND CLAY PARTICLES are an essential part of the soil. They are particularly needed near the surface where they help the delicate roots of young plants to meet less resistance from the coarser particles, lumps and pebbles.

6. Soil analysis

THE COARSER PARTICLES, including sand, play their part by preventing the finer silt and clay particles from clogging together to form a heavy, waterlogged soil. But, too high a proportion of sand means that the soil will be loose and moisture will drain away too fast, taking the soil nutrients with it. Sandy soils are therefore often called hungry soils, because they need so much feeding for the constant replacement of these nutrients.

THE LARGEST SOIL PARTICLES AND PEBBLES act as a useful form of soil drainage, although the really large pebbles and stones should be raked away and removed from plant-growing areas.

The favourite soil of gardeners and, indeed, the best soil of all, is made up from a mixture of humus, fine silt and clay particles together with coarser sand particles. It is called loam. Most garden plants do well in good, rich, loamy soils but some are more particular about the basic type of soil in which they will grow.

THE BASIC TYPES OF SOIL

Generally speaking, soils fall into two basic types: those that tend to be naturally acid and those that are more alkaline. Those that are balanced between are known as neutral. Whether soils are acid or alkaline depends entirely on their origins. If you live, for example, near sandy, peat-covered moorlands or commons, the soil is likely to be acid. If, on the other hand, you live, say, on the South Downs, the Cotswolds, or in parts of Yorkshire, where the underlying rock is chalk or limestone, your soil is likely to be more alkaline.

It is best for children to find out if their garden soil is basically acid or alkaline before buying or trying any special plants, as there are a few groups that are fussy about the type of soil in which they grow. Among the groups of plants that dislike growing in alkaline soils are such favourites as rhododendrons, camellias, gentians and most of the heaths and heathers. These are all acid-soil lovers and should not be tried in alkaline conditions unless they are planted in specially constructed raised beds, or in containers, filled with suitable acid soil. Various simple soil-testing kits can be bought from chemists, nurseries or garden centres to give an idea of whether soils in different areas tend towards being slightly acid or slightly alkaline. These tests can be carried out by young gardeners under adult supervision and the results are usually shown on a scale such as this:

pH5	pH6	pH7	pH8	pH9
slightly acid		neutral		slightly alkaline

pH is a chemical term used to define the acidity or alkalinity of the soil.

SPECIAL BOUGHT SOILS

Bags of growing-media, growing-composts, bought from garden centres or shops can be useful for various gardening purposes. Many different ready-prepared and sterilised types are available and these are especially useful for seedpans and boxes for growing seedlings and larger plants, as well as for pots or other containers, especially those used for indoor plants. Here is a list of some of the best-known types which are available from stores, seedsmen, nurseries and garden centres:

SOIL-BASED   The John Innes (JI) types which consist of loam, silver sand
and fertiliser.

JI Seed Compost for seeds and cuttings

JI No 1 for potting-on young seedlings and rooted cuttings

JI No 2, the standard growing compost for most potted plants, which
contains twice as much fertiliser as JI No 1

JI No 3, for plants which need high nutrient levels, which contains
twice as much fertiliser as JI No 2

PEAT-BASED   Levington seed compost

Levington potting compost

J. Arthur Bowers general potting compost

J. Arthur Bowers lime-free compost for azaleas, camellias, etc

J. Arthur Bowers cactus compost

Rochford's house plant compost

Try not to let these composts dry out as they are difficult to wet again.

FEEDING

Feeding the soil means ensuring that there is plenty of humus in it and
adding nutrients in the form of fertilisers. These improve the nutrient
content of the soil and replace those nutrients removed by plants. Try to
buy fertilisers made from natural organic materials such as bonemeal,
hoof and horn, compound fish manures or seaweed.

Many gardeners prefer to buy these natural fertilisers rather than
artificial types because they believe that vegetables and fruit taste better
and are more nourishing when they are grown organically. These organic
fertilisers put back waste plant and animal materials into the soil and help
to counteract the depletion of the earth's natural resources. For further
information write to the Henry Doubleday Research Association, referred
to on p. 166.

WATERING

This is sometimes essential in dry weather and particularly so for seedlings and freshly bedded-out plants which may not have established
sufficient root growth to link them into their new surroundings. It is also
necessary for small, shallow-rooted plants that are growing in fast-
draining soils. Light, sandy or gravelly soils do not hold moisture as long
as the loamy mixtures of sand, clay and humus. Rainwater should be used
wherever possible.

Larger plants with roots that go down a long way do not need water, except in very long periods of drought. In fact, in the summer it is often difficult to know whether to water or not. It is impossible to make general rules, but it should be remembered that plants cannot survive without water and so it is important to be sure that they have an adequate supply in the soil.

Plants that are producing flowers use a lot of water and so do fast-growing plants. An unceasing supply of moisture in the soil enables the green leaves of such fast-growing plants as runner beans to stay firm, turgid and healthy. This means that they can perform the function of photosynthesis, or the building-up of simple foods with the help of sunlight, uninterruptedly, and so continue growing.

There are dangers in both under and overwatering but it is better to give plants a long and thorough soaking less often than frequent 'top-wetting' sprinklings. The motto here should always be 'soak, not splash'. The frequent, small applications encourage the plants to throw out roots too near the surface, which then suffer from scorch in the hot sun. These roots will be produced at the expense of those at lower levels, so denying the plants access to water which is stored there after rain. When the earth is soaked to a depth of 60–90 cm (2–3 ft) at each watering the plants' roots go on growing normally.

When using a hose for watering, children should place the nozzle close to the plants' stems so that the soil is not disturbed. They should not use the spraying rose of a hose or watering can except for settling the soil after planting. Plants should never be watered while the sun is shining on them, otherwise drops, which will act like magnifying glasses, may be left on the flowers or leaves, thus intensifying the sun's heat and burning the plants.

MULCHING

Moisture in the soil can be conserved, and weeds kept down, by mulching. This involves spreading a 7·5 cm (3 in) layer of peat, garden compost, bark fibre, ripe dung or even grass cuttings, on the surface of the soil. Rain soaks through this layer taking nourishment with it to the soil below. At the same time, the mulch prevents water evaporating from the soil, especially near the surface.

Mulches should not be applied too close to the plants' stems or they may rot them. They should be lightly forked into the top of the soil from time to time and a fresh layer applied. A mulch should always be put down on top of damp soil. A prickly mulch of chopped-up holly, gorse or thistle leaves and stems over a row of newly sown seeds, such as peas, helps to protect them from mice and birds which might otherwise dig them out.

WEEDS

Weeds are sometimes defined as any plants which are growing where they are not wanted in the garden. They are usually thought of as wild flowers but technically a weed could be a seedling of any cultivated plant that is growing in the wrong place. Some of these wild invaders have most attractive flowers and will be an asset to the garden, but where they overcrowd cultivated flowers and vegetables and compete with them for

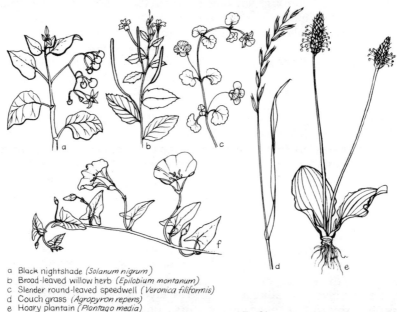

a Black nightshade *(Solanum nigrum)*
b Broad-leaved willow herb *(Epilobium montanum)*
c Slender round-leaved speedwell *(Veronica filiformis)*
d Couch grass *(Agropyron repens)*
e Hoary plantain *(Plantago media)*
f Lesser bindweed *(Convolvulus arvensis)*

7. Six common garden weeds

soil moisture and sunlight they should be removed. This is particularly important in the vegetable garden as the plants will be unable to grow properly and produce good crops when overrun with weeds.

Some people destroy the weeds in their gardens by spraying them with weed-killers. This practice—although at first sight it may appear to be easier than digging them out or pulling them up—is a great waste, for even big weeds, with some important exceptions, can be useful for making garden compost (see Appendix I). These poisonous sprays will also harm any wildlife which is sharing our gardens with us.

TOOLS

Anyone, at any age no matter how young, deserves to have good tools, and these should be carefully looked after from the start. Children should never be fobbed off with toy spades or other implements made from inferior materials. All tools that are bought, rather than inherited as so many often are, should be the best that can be afforded, preferably made by a well-known firm. Nowadays many stainless-steel implements can be obtained; they are initially expensive, but last longer than others. If these are too costly, those made from forged steel with light and strong synthetic or wooden handles will be satisfactory. Handle height should be taken into account when choosing tools. Often what are called ladies' spades and forks are short enough for young gardeners, but in all cases choose lightweight tools which feel well balanced, discarding any that are heavy in the head.

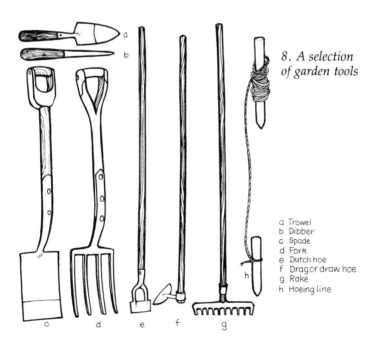

8. A selection of garden tools

a Trowel
b Dibber
c Spade
d Fork
e Dutch hoe
f Drag or draw hoe
g Rake
h Hoeing line

Here is a list of the basic tools needed by the young gardener:

SPADE   For deeper digging, lifting out and moving chunks of soil.

FORK   For breaking and turning the soil. A fork is not so good for lifting as the earth goes through the open tines when it is moved. Both spades and forks should be put into the soil surface at an upright angle and pressed down with one foot, as deep as is necessary, before being levered up. It is best to dig only about 12·5–15 cm (5–6 in) deep at a time. Slightly different types of handles for both tools are shown in Fig. 8.

HOE   For working the soil surface, breaking it up, loosening young weeds (older, deep-rooted weeds need digging out) and generally keeping it aerated. Different types of hoe are shown in Fig. 8.

RAKE   For tidying the surface of the soil, raking off fallen leaves, loose weeds and even unwanted pebbles. A rake can also be used to break up smallish lumps of soil by turning it end on and just using a corner. Stiff bamboo-strip or wire rakes, with long, bent prongs, are useful for gathering up leaves and cut grass from lawns.

TROWEL   For planting out bulbs and bedding-out plants, to make holes to put them into and also for digging out plants that are to be transplanted. A gardener's trowel can become a very personal implement, almost like an extension of a hand.

DIBBER   Also for planting out. This is a smoothly pointed part of an old fork or spade-shaft which includes the handle. It makes regular-shaped holes which are needed for some big seeds, leek plants, etc.

HOEING-LINE   Sometimes also known as a pegging-, row-making or seed-sowing line, it is a length of cord, slightly longer than the width of the plot, tied firmly at each end to two strong sticks. When the cord is taut and the sticks placed strongly into the earth, a straight line can be neatly hoed between them.

HOSE AND WATERING CAN   For watering.

SECATEURS   For cutting back and pruning plants.

WHEELBARROW   For moving garden materials, including rubbish and compost.

The list of basic tools required for gardening can obviously be augmented by others. Lawn mowers are essential for those with lawns and hedge-clippers for those with hedges or a number of large shrubs. Children should not be allowed to use any electrical equipment, nor should they be within reach of such tools as sickles or garden scythes until they are skilled and old enough to realise their dangers.

Most experienced gardeners manage with a minimum of tools which they keep in good condition by looking after them carefully. Children should always make sure that any implements they have used are cleaned, dried and have their blades lightly oiled to prevent them from corroding. Tools should never be left lying about but should be stood up or, better still, hung up in a dry place, heads uppermost.

Greenhouses and cloches

A greenhouse, if it is available, can be useful to encourage the young gardener to grow plants that need some protection from the weather. Many of the tender (not frost hardy) seedlings can be grown initially under glass as the unexposed soil, even when there is no heat in the greenhouse, is warmer and there is no risk of cold wind, freezing air or soil surface, or even cold summer nights, damaging the plants. If there is a greenhouse in the garden, it should be kept very clean and a careful note should be made of the night temperatures to see if they are high enough for some of the more exotic plants to be grown.

Thousands of gardeners manage without greenhouses and bring on their crops early in rather primitive frames, made from concrete blocks or stacked bricks, their tops covered with thick polythene or glass. In warmer parts of the country cloches, made from glass or polythene, give good protection for winter salads in the form of lettuce, corn salad, landcress and parsley (see Chapter 5). These could also be used by children to bring on early crops by covering rows sown in the vegetable garden. Here the polythene hoop types are easier and safer to use than the older glass ones which can cause injuries, even when carefully handled by adults.

GARDENING NOTEBOOK

1. Make short notes and careful sketches of the different soil-analysis tests you have done. Draw the widths of the different layers as accurately as you can and colour them in, making sure that you add a key. Label each sketch with the place where the soil was collected and the names of the plants growing there and decide, from the widths of the different layers, the main characteristics of the soil.
2. Look at the weeds growing in your garden. Try to identify them from a wild-flower book (see p. 161) and either draw or press the flowers. The ones growing in your garden can be picked as they will have to be removed anyway but leave those that are growing in the countryside.

3. Collect and mount leaflets on organic fertilisers, for reference (see p. 166 for addresses of some firms to which you could write).
4. Write up the results of any soil acidity and alkalinity tests that you do, noting down any plants that will not grow in your garden because of this.
5. Make a note of any watering that is done in the garden, explaining why it is necessary.
6. Make a montage of garden-tool pictures and, if they are only printed in black and white, colour them in.

FURTHER TOPICS FOR DISCUSSION, OBSERVATION AND RESEARCH

1. The fine ash left from bonfires or incinerators used to burn otherwise useless plant material is a source of a valuable substance known as potash. This ash should be spread out over the surface of the garden as soon as is possible and eventually dug in. Discuss the problems of burning garden rubbish and the precautions that can be taken to do it safely.
2. Weeds are the most successful plants in the world. Why do you think this is? Do they survive hard weather? Do they produce many seeds? Find out more about weeds and make drawings of their seeds. The wind blows some about; look out for dandelion clocks and notice how each seed has its own parachute.
3. Look at the different types of soil throughout the country and try to find out what is the underlying rock. Samples of different soils and rocks could be collected and drawings made of the layers of the earth's crust seen in exposed cliff faces or excavations. Notice, too, the different plants which are growing on these various soils.
4. Find out more about peat in the public library. Scientists are discovering information about the history of some creatures and plants and their pollen from the remains that have been preserved in good, fossilised peat beds in different parts of the country.

4 · Propagating plants

Plant propagation, growing new plants from seed, or vegetatively from part of the parent plant's established growth, is both fascinating and rewarding for gardeners of all ages. For children it can be especially so because it gives them a tremendous sense of achievement and may often spark off their interest in all other aspects of gardening, leading to completely new interests.

If carried out carefully, seed-growing and most vegetative propagation techniques can be successful but it is vital that young gardeners follow the basic rules and look after their plants conscientiously. The production of a young plant is by no means the end of the story as it has to be tended carefully until it has become well established, and after that too, if it is to prosper and grow.

Plants in the wild reproduce themselves (and ensure their continuation) in two basic ways—by seed and/or vegetatively by producing new plantlets year by year from the parent, often at the end of long shoots which bend down to the soil and take root, or by winter buds of some kind. Many garden plants also reproduce themselves in these ways but some hybrids and cultivars (see p. 75) that have been specially cultivated by man seldom set seed and so cannot reproduce themselves like this. Gardeners can increase their stock of these plants by using vegetative methods.

Children should look out for self-sown seedlings and notice carefully how far they are from their parent plants.

PROPAGATION FROM SEED

Flower and vegetable seeds can be bought in packets from seedsmen, or they can be collected and saved from gardens. Each fertile seed contains a tiny new plant, or embryo, and food reserves for its initial growth. These are both enclosed in an outer skin, or testa, which will be ruptured when germination starts. If some different seeds are examined (and the bigger they are the easier they are to see), it is possible to make out that the embryos have seed leaves, or cotyledons, a shoot, or plumule, and an immature root, or radicle.

The food reserve may be stored in the cotyledons, especially if they are fat and fleshy, or in the tissue that surrounds the embryo. This reserve is used for the initial growth of the young plant, until the root and shoot have grown enough to start performing their natural functions in food manufacture. It is the green leaves, that grow as the shoot develops, which can manufacture food from water, air and sunlight, by a process known as photosynthesis. The water is taken into the plant from the soil by the hairs near the tips of the roots. Food reserves in the seed include starches, proteins, some vitamins and minute amounts of mineral trace elements needed for growth. The larger the seedling to be produced, the

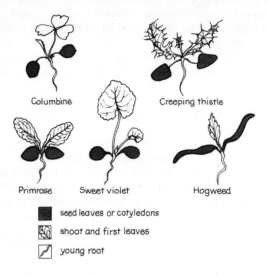

Columbine   Creeping thistle

Primrose   Sweet violet   Hogweed

■ seed leaves or cotyledons

▨ shoot and first leaves

▧ young root

9. The development of seedlings

larger the food reserves must be, so it is the larger seeds, like peas and beans, with nutritious cotyledons, that are often used to provide food for humans too.

There is frequently some confusion about the definition of two words used by botanists—seed and fruit. A seed is the product of one fertilised ovule. The persisting and often enveloping remains of one flower, when the seeds are ripe, is called the fruit. An example, again using the pea or bean, is that the whole pod is known as the fruit, which contains several seeds—the peas or beans.

Seeds develop, once a flower has been pollinated and fertilisation has occurred (see p. 30), in many kinds of containers which may have, for example, thick, thin, fleshy, smooth or hooked outer skins. 'Seed-boxes', which is a loose, but popular, name for fruits, vary enormously and much interest can be gained by looking for the various shapes and kinds (see Fig. 25) and by observing the ways in which they open to disperse the seed. As the final success of a plant relies on producing ripe and viable seeds, it is important that these should be dispersed as efficiently as possible. Some, such as dandelions, have parachute attachments and can be blown about; some, such as lupins, split when they are ripe; some, like the giant balsam, even explode (see Fig. 14) and others, for example poppies, merely have pores or holes through which the seeds escape. Children enjoy looking out for the different methods by which plants try to ensure that their seeds disperse and reach the soil.

The seeds produced by a plant in the autumn do not always germinate immediately they are ripe, or even when they reach the ground. Some of them rest, or stay dormant, through the winter until conditions for their initial and continued growth are better. It is interesting that some seeds have inbuilt inhibiting factors which delay germination until temperature and other conditions are just right for their growth.

Collecting ripe seed from growing plants is fun for young gardeners (see p. 60), but they need to be shown the importance of keeping each kind in a separate packet. Packets should be labelled immediately and it is a good idea to stick on pictures, photographs or cut-outs from old catalogues, of the plants they will grow into. They could also add short notes, obtained from books or from seed packets seen in shops, for sowing the seeds and growing the plants on. The collected seed must be stored in dry places which are frost- and mouse-proof.

Germination will only take place in moist, warm conditions. As the seeds absorb moisture their food reserves are converted into simple plant sugars and amino-acids and they produce extra vitamins, all of which enable the young embryonic root to start growing and begin to supply the tiny plant with enough water and further nutrients. Soon the shoots begin developing and they lengthen and expand, often still protected by the cotyledons. Seedling shoots vary greatly. Some cotyledons act as first leaves; they are green, come up above the soil and help to begin to manufacture food themselves. There are a few pictures of young plants in Fig. 9 showing how their cotyledons spread out and give the seedlings a start as the shoot grows. The cotyledons frequently look quite different in shape from the first and subsequent true leaves and are distinguished in the drawing by shading.

Children can learn a great deal about the growth of seeds by starting a few off temporarily in water, as described in Chapter 11. Different types, including perhaps a bean, some mustard seed, a maize grain and a few grains of barley, can be easily watched through the sides of a jam jar (see Fig. 30). A lining of blotting paper should be placed in the jar and the central well filled with damp sand. The seed should then be 'planted' between the glass and the blotting paper, and the sand kept moist all the time. In this way the various stages of seedling growth, or germination, can be observed and the fact that the bean and mustard have two cotyledons and the maize and barley only one should be pointed out.

When seed is bought, children should at first only buy small quantities at a time, until they have a better idea of how much they need. It is a false economy to buy too much and hope that the excess will do for the next year, as seed (particularly that from specially cultivated plants) can easily deteriorate while it is stored and only a very few seedlings may germinate in seasons after the date on the packet. As seed is fairly inexpensive, it should be bought fresh each year to avoid disappointment in the amount which germinates.

Seeds of many vegetables and flowers can now be bought in pelleted form; each of the seeds is surrounded by a coating-material which contains some fertiliser. The coating makes them bigger and easier to handle and it also acts as a protective layer. When the seeds come into contact with moisture the coating breaks down and germination continues in the normal way.

Seed sowing

When the time is right for sowing seeds it must be remembered that they need moisture and warmth to enable them to germinate. They also require fresh air, but many of them do better in darkness. Their covering should vary in depth, according to their type, and a light sprinkling of soil or seed-sowing compost is enough for some small seeds. A rather vague idea exists that seeds need a covering equal to the measurement of their widest part, but this may be inadequate for a protection from probing birds. On the other hand, it is important to take care that they are not sown too deeply or their food reserves may be exhausted before the shoot reaches the surface. However, the instructions on the packets should be followed exactly, as professional seedsmen have many years' experience behind them and certainly know best.

For outdoor seed sowing the ground should be carefully prepared. It should be dug over thoroughly and compost or manure should be added before it is left to 'weather' through the winter. Exposure to frost helps to break up the soil. Before the seeds are sown, and when the weather is warm and dry enough, the surface should be raked over to break up large lumps of soil and remove any stones. The object is to obtain a surface of fine soil, the tilth, into which the seeds can be sown. Once this is produced the soil can be firmed (most easily done by treading carefully over the whole surface) and then given a thorough soaking with the rose attachment on a watering can or hose. Some people stand on a wooden portable board or plank when they are working on the soil, moving it along as they finish each stretch. Others prefer standing on the earth and this practice is not harmful as dry earth needs firming down again before the rows can be made for sowing.

Seeds of some plants, including tender flowering plants and some vegetables, are best sown in shallow containers in a greenhouse, frame or indoors on a windowsill. The seedlings are grown on until they are large enough and the weather sufficiently mild for them to be pricked out (see p. 55) or planted out into the garden. A wide variety of containers can be used for seed sowing, including standard and half-size seed trays, the latter useful for smaller quantities. Small pots made from peat and others made from a specially prepared biodegradable material, often known as whalehide, can be helpful in the case of larger individual seeds, as both types can be 'planted' straight out into open ground and will gradually rot away, leaving an undisturbed seedling which will go on growing. Shallow flower pots with drainage holes, or similar containers of earthenware or plastic, can also be used for seed sowing.

The soil or other growing-medium into which the seeds are sown must be airy and well drained and contain plenty of sand. There are now several special seed-sowing composts on the market (see p. 41) which have been specifically formulated to give these characteristics. The containers should be filled to within 1 cm (about ½ in) of the top and the compost firmed down well. It should then be watered with a watering can fitted with a fine rose attachment.

Once the seed has been sown the containers can be covered with glass or plastic and brown paper or newspaper. This helps control moisture loss, provides darker conditions and lessens the need for watering, and for some species the warm, humid conditions are vital for successful germination.

VEGETABLES Vegetable seed is best sown out of doors in rows to make weeding and handling the plants easier. Use a hoeing- or pegging-line (see Fig. 8) to mark straight lines across the plot, according to the plan already drawn up (see p. 65). A drill, a small furrow into which seeds are sown, of the appropriate depth should be taken out with the corner of a hoe or a trowel.

The seed packet should be opened carefully, tearing off one corner, and some seeds trickled into the palm of the hand. The seeds should then be sown thinly along the drill, taking a small pinch between finger and thumb. Using a rake, the seeds can then be covered by drawing soil from the sides of the drill over them and then the surface should be firmed by treading down the rows. The ends of the rows should be marked with a stick or plastic label over which the empty seed packet can be slipped and covered with a tied plastic bag to identify the individual crops.

FLOWERS   The position in the garden where flower seeds are sown will depend upon whether the plant is an annual, biennial or perennial (see pp. 78–81), and a sun or shade lover. Hardy annuals can be sown directly in their final positions and in this case it is usually better to scatter, or broadcast, the seed over an area rather than sowing it in drills which will look too formal. The young gardener could plan out a 'patchwork' of different annual plants in one part of a border using species with different coloured flowers, or those of similar shades. The areas for each type should be marked with string and pegs before seed is sown. Half-hardy annuals, on the other hand, should be sown in pots in the greenhouse or house and then planted out when the weather becomes warmer. Seed of biennial and perennial plants is usually sown in drills and then the larger plants put into their final positions later. In all cases the same method of sowing as described above should be followed.

Where seed is to be saved from plants the whole fruiting heads should be cut off in late summer or autumn when they are ripe. They should be placed on paper-lined trays in a greenhouse or sunny window for a week or so, when the seed can be rubbed or shaken out and packeted. If hybrids or cultivars set seed they can be saved and will often give a mixed population of seedlings—some may be like one parent, some like the other, while the rest need not have any visible likenesses. These plants may not breed true from seed and can give added interest as their development is watched.

TREES AND SHRUBS   Propagating trees and shrubs by seed is certainly not the quickest way to produce large plants and if these are required the vegetative methods described later are better. However, children will find seed propagation interesting and will obtain a great sense of achievement as the plant grows. Some seedsmen sell packets of tree and shrub seeds but the most exciting way is to collect seeds from trees and shrubs already growing. There is not much literature available for amateur gardeners on propagating the different wild and cultivated trees and shrubs from seed but there are several basic rules that can be followed, as explained in Chapter 9.

A few berries from different plants, such as *Berberis, Cotoneaster* and *Rosa* species, that the birds have not taken for food, can be harvested when ripe in the autumn and stored outside in shallow sand-filled boxes, which must be protected from mice. This helps the flesh of the berries to decay and hastens subsequent germination by exposing the seeds to a period of low temperatures. In the spring the seed should be separated or sieved out and sown in drills outside or in pots indoors. Seeds of other trees and shrubs could also be collected and stored and sown as described.

Thinning out

When seeds have been sown outside in their final positions, either in drills or broadcast over an area, the seedlings will need to be thinned out. No matter how thinly the seeds have been sown there will not be room for all plants to come to maturity and yield a crop, or flower well, because there will be too much competition between the seedlings for light and water. When the seedlings are touching each other and beginning to look crowded the weakest looking plants should be taken out so that the remainder are spaced to the distance recommended on the seed packet. With many vegetables, such as carrots, the thinnings, immature plants, can be eaten in salads and it is common practice to thin out in two stages, to half the required spacing in the first stage and then later thinning again. The discarded plants should not be left on the ground, where they may become diseased and affect the growing plants, but, like other waste material, should be put on the compost heap.

Transplanting

Similarly, when seeds have been sown in rows or pots which are not to be their final locations the seedlings must be spaced out to give the plants room to develop. Biennials and perennials should be transplanted carefully, taking care not to damage the roots, to another part of the garden, where they have space to go on growing, and finally be watered in well. Seedlings grown in containers in the house or greenhouse should be spaced several centimetres apart in rows in seed trays or small pots containing seed-sowing compost. This should be done when the first true leaves develop and great care is needed to avoid damaging the tender young roots and shoots. This latter operation is known as pricking out and when the plants are becoming too large for this position they can be planted outside as directed on the seed packet.

VEGETATIVE PROPAGATION

As mentioned earlier this method can give a quicker means of producing larger plants than that of growing them from seed and it can be just as much fun for children. Basically the techniques involve taking parts of plants already grown in the garden, or given by other people from their gardens, and encouraging them to root and become separate, new, growing plants. There are several different methods, the choice of which will depend on the plant's growth habit. This type of propagation ensures that the new plant will have exactly the same characteristics as the parent, whereas seeds may produce a mixed population with only some parts resembling the parent. When a clone is referred to by gardeners, it means that all the plants were originally produced from a single individual and cultivated and maintained vegetatively since.

Cuttings

In the majority of cases cuttings represent the easiest and quickest method of propagation. Stem cuttings are the most commonly used but the term can also refer to the removal of portions from the plant's leaves and roots. It is best to remove suitable cutting material from the plants with secateurs and then bring it indoors to trim it up. A very sharp knife is needed for this trimming up, so adults should either carry out this task themselves or supervise it very closely.

STEM CUTTINGS can be taken from side shoots or from the main shoot of most shrubs and trees. Depending on the age of the shoot they are known as hardwood, semi-ripe or softwood cuttings.

Hardwood cuttings, taken in the autumn or early spring, are the most foolproof method of propagating the majority of common shrubs and many trees. They can be used for subjects like forsythia and roses. Shoots which have grown in the previous summer and become woody are cut 20–25 cm (8–10 in) long. The cut should be made just below a bud or with a portion of the main stem (or heel) in the case of side shoots. The base of the cutting should be prepared with a straight, sharp cut and then dipped in hormone rooting powder to encourage the formation of roots. The cuttings can then be placed in the garden in a narrow trench which has a layer of coarse sand in the bottom, firmed well and left in position for up to a year to root.

Semi-ripe, or semi-hardwood cuttings are taken in the summer or early autumn from the shoots of the current season's growth which are hardening at the base. They should be 10–20 cm (4–8 in) long and should be cut just below a bud or pulled off carefully with a heel of wood. The lower leaves should be removed and the base of the cutting dipped into hormone rooting powder. Some kind of propagator is useful for this type of cutting.

Softwood cuttings are taken from the young growing tips of shrubs, herbaceous, house, and greenhouse plants in the summer. They can be used for plants like geraniums, chrysanthemums and most others. Since both leaves and stems are very young these cuttings have to be handled carefully—they lose moisture quickly and so need warm, humid conditions for rooting. These conditions could be achieved in a propagating frame, either bought or home-made, consisting of a tray of compost with a rigid plastic high cover, or a pot of compost covered by a polythene bag supported on sticks. In all cases the cover must be airtight so that high levels of humidity are maintained, although it is a good idea to open the covers for a very few minutes daily to refresh the air.

Non-flowering shoots 5–10 cm (2–4 in) long should be cut below a leaf joint, or node. The bottom two pairs of leaves should be removed, the base of this nodal cutting dipped into hormone rooting powder and then inserted firmly in the growing medium. This should be light and open in texture—either lime-free sharp sand or an equal mixture of sand and peat. The medium should then be kept moist until the cuttings have rooted. Special bought seed-sowing composts (see p. 41) can also be used for rooting cuttings.

Herbaceous plants can be propagated from stem cuttings taken in early spring. These cuttings can be taken from young shoots when 7·5–10 cm (3–4 in) long and the cut made below soil level if possible, as long as they are firm and solid at the base. They should be trimmed cleanly below a joint and inserted into sandy soil in a frame or outside. Suitable herbaceous plants which can be propagated by this method include lupin, delphinium, scabious, coreopsis and phlox.

LEAF CUTTINGS can be used to propagate many house plants, such as African violet and bryophyllum (see Fig. 28), begonia, gloxinia, streptocarpus and echeveria, and a large number of new plants can be obtained in this way. A few leaves with their leaf stems attached should be removed from the parent plant and should be inserted into pure sand or a sandy compost. Young plantlets will form at the blade end of the leaf where it joins the stem. *Begonia rex* has large leaves which can be laid on the surface of the compost and cuts made across the veins. A pebble or hairgrip can be used to hold the leaf down, making sure that the cut vein is in contact with the compost; this is important as that is where the young plantlets will form. This method can also be used with *Streptocarpus*, and in both cases leaves can also be cut into squares and inserted into the compost to produce new plantlets. It is essential to make sure that the leaf pieces are put in the right way up, with the lower edge in the soil. Leaves of mother-in-law's tongue (*Sansevieria trifasciata*) can also be encouraged to produce plantlets when they are cut up into pieces 5–7·5 cm (2–3 in) long and inserted into the compost the same way up as they grew. Propagation of indoor plants is discussed further in Chapter 11.

ROOT CUTTINGS are particularly suitable for increasing plants with thick, fleshy roots. Herbaceous plants which can be propagated in this way include phlox, gaillardia, anchusa, hollyhock, verbascum, oriental poppy and statice, but not gypsophila or lupin. A complete plant should be lifted during the winter and the roots cut into pieces 2·5–5 cm (1–2 in) long. They should be inserted in the compost, the right way up, using different cuts to distinguish the top from the bottom. Thin cuttings, from plants such as phlox, can be laid horizontally on the compost and covered with 1 cm (½ in) of soil.

With all cuttings, once roots have formed and developed, the new plants can be transplanted into pots to grow on if they are not large enough to be planted out in the garden.

Division

This is an obvious and simple method of increasing plants which have fibrous roots and grow from many crowns. This method is most usually used for herbaceous plants, such as Michaelmas daisies, phlox, helenium and golden rod and involves obtaining a piece of shoot with roots that are already growing from it.

To divide heavy, old perennial clumps, the whole plant should be lifted in the autumn by two people, each with a fork, one on either side, so that the roots are disturbed as little as possible. The plant should not be chopped up with spades, as used to be recommended, but instead the best of the young offshoots should be separated, complete with their roots, by hand or with a knife if necessary. These should be replanted carefully, allowing room for the roots' natural spread, then fine soil should be put in the hole so that all the spaces are filled. Finally, the soil should be pressed and firmed down with the fingertips and then by treading all round.

Some trees and shrubs which produce many suckers or shoots close to the ground can also be propagated in this way, as can some of the alpines and rockery plants. It should be carried out in the spring, or after flowering if the plants bloom in the spring. Lilacs and roses produce many suckers but, if these have been grafted or budded originally themselves, (see p. 59), they will be from the basal rootstock and will grow differently from the shrub now in the garden. In this case another propagation method, for example, cuttings, should be tried instead. Because of this difference in growth, the suckers, which only impoverish a plant's growth, should always be removed from the base of rose and special lilac bushes.

Layering

Trees and shrubs in particular can be propagated by layering and this often occurs naturally with sprawling shrubs whose lower branches sweep down on to the ground. However, to induce branches to send out stem, or adventitious, roots and layer, a one-year-old shoot near the ground should be chosen and an upward cut should be made halfway through it, just below a leaf joint, or node. This shoot, with the cut kept open carefully, should then be pegged down on the soil and covered so that at least 10 cm (4 in) on each side of the cut is buried under damp soil. It may take some months for the stem roots to develop, so the layer should be left for quite some time before it is checked for roots. This technique can be used for many ornamental shrubs, such as rhododendrons, quinces and climbing plants, like honeysuckles, as well as for strawberries, loganberries and blackberries.

Layering is also possible above the ground. A healthy one-year-old branch should be selected and cut in the same way. Damp sphagnum moss should then be used to keep the cut open and to surround it, and should be covered with polythene which is taped firmly around the stem above and below the cut. The new roots can sometimes be seen among the moss inside the polythene as they develop. This technique is known as air layering and can be used for rhododendrons and also to produce a smaller leafy specimen of an indoor rubber plant which has become too tall and lost all its bottom leaves.

With both these methods a hormone rooting powder will speed root formation. Once roots have formed and are well established the new plant can be separated from the parent and planted out.

Grafting and budding

These two propagating techniques are more difficult to carry out than those previously mentioned and are used by professional gardeners. Grafting involves a cut stem of one plant (the scion) being inserted into the stem of another growing plant (the stock or rootstock). Budding is similar but only a small piece of scion tissue, a bud and a small section of stem, is inserted into the stem of the stock plant.

These propagation methods have several applications and they are most commonly used on fruit trees and roses. They are a means of imparting the characteristics of one parent to another, for example dwarfing rootstocks can be used to restrict the extension growth but not the fruiting of apple trees, or to overcome the inability of the scion plant to root from cuttings. Both techniques are relatively complex, requiring precise work, and are not really suitable for children to attempt, but they may be interested to know of them.

GARDENING NOTEBOOK

1. Start laying out two pages ready for your planting records, one for flowering plants and the other for vegetable sowing and planting. Rule at least six columns and head them: 1. Date, 2. Name of plant, 3. Method of sowing, 4. Time taken for full growth, 5. Comments on habits of growth, 6. Other remarks.

2. Add dated records of all your propagation activities to the planting diary, leaving room for further dated records of growth, plus comments.

3. Collect, draw and colour as many different seeds and 'seed-boxes' as you can. Some may be on trees in parks, so that they cannot be taken until they fall, but others may be on waste ground beside streets or on road-construction sites. Try always to look at the parent plants as you collect them. For weeds and wildflowers it is a good idea to take an identification book with you (see p. 161) so that you can try to identify the plants that have produced the seed.

4. Look out for berries and also study the chart of poisonous plants (available from RoSPA (see p. 167)) so that these can be avoided. Watch berried trees in autumn to see if they are visited by hungry birds and make notes about any that you see.

5. Look out for seedlings in the garden, allotment or park. Examine them closely while they are growing and notice if their stems come straight up through the surface of the ground, or if they are bent over in a crook-shape. Do the cotyledons still show, and are they green? Draw as many as you can and add the date when they were noticed.

6. After taking cuttings, or propagating plants in other ways, make notes in your own words of what you did. These will be useful for future reference so leave room for additional comments on the results of your efforts. Also make a note of any other ways in which the plant could have been propagated.

7. Look in the public library for some books about flowers and vegetables. If you find them interesting start a booklist of your own, after studying the one on p. 162.

FURTHER TOPICS FOR DISCUSSION, OBSERVATION AND RESEARCH

1. Have a discussion about seed food reserves. It is possible to test some of these substances and to identify them simply. Ask at the public library for an elementary book on biology which will give you some information on this subject.

2. Look up the word 'photosynthesis' in a big dictionary and also

'chlorophyll', then try to find out how plants without green colouring in their leaves manage to survive.

3. Study some of the weeds that are common in the area in which you live and try to find out some of the reasons why they spread so fast and do so well. Do they produce a lot of seed? Or is their seed dispersal method particularly good? Or do they increase vegetatively?

4. Look out for patches of wild blackberries and briars, or wild roses. The first produce long, arching stems which bend over so that their tips touch the ground and take root. Briars and other plants produce a mass of young shoot growth (or suckers) from their roots. They also produce seed, so they are doubly efficient. Look out for other plants that produce both new young plants and seed; coltsfoot and rosebay willow-herb are two more that spread both by seed and vegetatively.

5 · The vegetable and fruit garden

No vegetables ever taste as good as those that can be picked straight from the garden and they always seem even better, especially to children, if they have grown them themselves. Most of the tasks involved in vegetable growing will be within their capabilities.

The choice of vegetables and salad plants that it is possible to cultivate in a small plot is very wide. It depends, of course, on the amount of space available and individual tastes so it is best for children to spend some time carefully studying seed catalogues before any seeds are bought. Encourage them to be adventurous in their vegetable growing and to look out for new salad plants and for strange vegetables when they have a meal in a Chinese or Indian restaurant. The seeds of some of these are now available in this country, so children can find them in catalogues. Here are some useful and interesting vegetable and salad plants to try; they can all be grown easily.

ASPARAGUS PEAS have attractive purple-red flowers and small, winged pods. They crop heavily and the pods should be picked when young and eaten whole. Unlike the normal garden peas they do not need staking.
CARROTS are available in different shapes, long or stubby. The seed could be sown between rows of onions (see p. 68) and some young ones pulled to eat raw in salads.
GIANT SUNFLOWERS do better if they are started off indoors with one seed sown in each whalehide or peat pot (see p. 53). When planted out they grow quickly like Jack-and-the-Beanstalk plants, eventually producing soup-plate flower heads which the bees love. After pollination they develop into delicious crowns of edible seeds.
JERUSALEM ARTICHOKES are tall, rather sunflower-like plants which develop delicious tubers on their roots. The tubers can be dug up in the autumn and stored in sand for eating in the winter.
LANDCRESS is a leafy, rosette-forming salad plant which is similar to watercress but will grow on ground away from water.
LETTUCE should be sown in seed boxes first (see p. 53) and pricked out into final rows as soon as possible. The cultivars 'Little Gem' or 'Tom Thumb' should be tried if space is limited.
ONIONS AND SHALLOTS should both be grown from sets, or young

bulbs, as they are less likely to be attacked by onion fly than if grown from seed.

PERPETUAL SPINACH is one of the most useful of all vegetables as the plant keeps growing and picked leaves are soon replaced by others.

RADISHES are one of the quickest vegetables to grow and good for children to try initially as germination and subsequent development are rapid.

SWEET CORN OR MAIZE should be started off in the same way as the giant sunflowers and not put outside until all risks of frost are past. A warm, sheltered site is essential, especially in colder parts of the country.

The chart on p. 70 gives planting and harvesting times for most of the commonly grown vegetables so that children can plan when to sow their seeds.

PLANNING THE VEGETABLE PLOT

The space that has been set aside for vegetables should be measured and a plan of it can then be drawn to scale (see p. 65 where a suggested layout is shown). The rows of the chosen crops should be arranged with the shortest ones in front, or else the taller ones will overshadow them and take too much light. Young gardeners should study the seedsmen's lists to find out exactly how much room each individual plant needs. For example, they should understand that, although the seeds of Brussels sprouts and cabbages are very small, the fully grown plants will be large and will need to be planted 60 cm (2 ft) apart in their final positions. Again, onion sets must be planted at least 15 cm (6 in) apart. They should also remember to leave sufficient room to get in between the rows, both for picking and for hoeing while the plants are still growing.

PREPARATION

It is essential that the ground is very carefully prepared before any seed is sown, and the method is explained on p. 52. Successful cultivation of all plants depends very largely on a fine tilth being obtained before seeds are sown and this is especially important where vegetables are concerned, if the best possible results are to be achieved. Young gardeners will gain a special sense of achievement from growing their own food crops and they should, at an early stage, understand the importance of getting the soil right. Most of them are likely to enjoy the preparatory work involved.

SEED SOWING

Seeds must not be sown too early in the year—as they only rot in cold, wet soil before they can start germinating. Instead young enthusiasts should try to be patient and wait until more experienced gardeners in the district sow their vegetable seeds. Encourage children to talk to gardeners who have been growing successfully for years as most are only too happy to pass on hints and tips to keen youngsters.

To sow the seeds the plot should be marked out according to the plan which was made, using a hoeing- or pegging-line (see Fig. 8) to keep the rows straight. Seed should be sown and seedlings transplanted as described in Chapter 4, following the instructions on the seed packet. Tender seedlings, like those of marrows and courgettes, do well if they are put out into the top of compost heaps once the frosts are over. The heat generated by the heap will help the subsequent rapid growth of the plants but enough soil should be put on top ready for their roots to get a good start.

CROP SUCCESSION

To make maximum use of the space available the vegetable plot should be kept full during the growing season and then rested, where possible, during the worst of the winter. When one crop has been harvested another one should be ready to go in its place. Any remains of harvested plants should be cleared away carefully so that diseases do not spread and the ground should be re-composted, adding a top-dressing of fertiliser (see p. 42) before re-sowing, to give the growing plants the extra nourishment they need.

A good crop succession has different kinds of plants following each other so that nutrient levels in the soil remain balanced and specific pests are not allowed to build up. The three main vegetable groups for rotations are:

(A) greens, such as cabbage and sprouts
(B) root crops, such as carrots and potatoes
(C) other crops, including legumes, such as peas and beans, which are very useful as they help to add nitrogen to the soil.

Crops in each group should be put together and this is shown on the plan on p. 65. In the second and subsequent years the groups should be moved around (rotated) so that they do not occupy the same part of the plot for two years running.

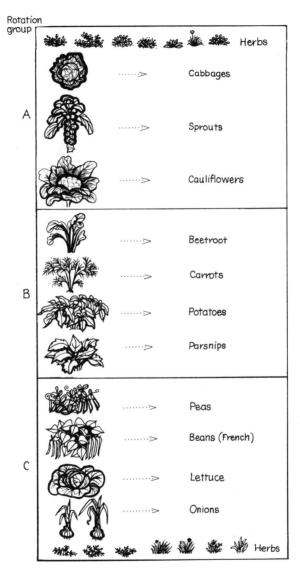

10. *A vegetable rotation plan*

HERBS

On the plan for a vegetable plot on p. 65 some culinary herbs have been included as suggested edging plants. Many of these flavouring herbs are perennials which means that they continue growing year after year and only need trimming or occasionally dividing into smaller plants (see p. 81) to keep them healthy and productive.

An unusual and attractive herb garden can be made using an old and unwanted ladder. This can be placed on the ground and separate herbs planted between each rung.

Rosemary   Chives   Fennel   Sage   Chamomile   Thyme

11. A herb garden grown in an old horizontal ladder

It is being more generally recognised now that herbs like ROSEMARY, LAVENDER, THYME, WINTER SAVORY and MINT (which are also called aromatic plants because of the fragrance of their leaves) may help in keeping unwanted insects and other small pests away from plants growing near them. This means that herbs not only are ornamental and useful in giving flavourings to salads and cooked food, but also have some protective value towards other plants.

The herbs most commonly grown are MINT, THYME and PARSLEY. MINT is a perennial which needs to be planted so that its growth is confined, otherwise its creeping stems will spread and root too extensively. It is quite a good idea to grow it in an old bottomless bucket with its rim sunk to soil level. PARSLEY, an annual, can be grown from seeds (which are said to be viable for only one year), although germination may take quite a long time. Tradition says that the seed should be sown on Good Friday but this rather depends on the time Easter occurs in the year. PARSLEY will sometimes seed itself. THYME is a perennial which makes a small, low shrub. It needs cutting back, unless it is being constantly picked, because otherwise the stems may elongate and the plant will produce fewer and fewer leaves.

There are plenty of other useful herbs which can be easily grown in gardens. Here are a few with interesting flavours:

BORAGE   An annual which has bright blue flowers which can be used to decorate salads or float on drinks. The young leaves can also be used to add flavour to salads.

GARLIC   A member of the onion family which has a very strong flavour. Fresh bulbs or cloves should be planted each autumn to produce more for the following year.

CHIVES   A perennial which also belongs to the onion family. It has narrow, tubular leaves which can be chopped to provide a mild onion taste for sandwiches, pâtés, soups and sauces.

SAGE   A perennial shrub with pungently aromatic leaves which give a spicy flavour to stuffings, soups and sauces. It should be used sparingly as it has a very strong flavour. Purple or red sage can be planted to add interesting colour to the garden.

ROSEMARY   Another perennial shrub which has pale blue flowers that can be added to salads and drinks. The leaves have a concentrated, outstanding flavour and have several uses, including being placed in cuts in the skin of roasting lamb.

FENNEL   A tall perennial which can be grown easily from seed. It has feathery leaves which taste of aniseed and are delicious chopped into a white sauce to use with some vegetables and fish.

TARRAGON   A perennial producing leaves which give a distinctive flavour to soups, stuffings and sauces. 'French' tarragon is said to have the best flavour.

Many of the herbs mentioned above produce flowers which attract bees into the garden. The annuals amongst them can be grown easily from seed and the perennials can be bought as young plants.

As well as being grown for culinary purposes, many herbs from gardens, and the countryside too, have been used through the ages for their medicinal properties. Some, for example, that produce fresh green leaves each spring, supplied people with extra vitamins long before it was recognised how essential these elements were. Others have been specified for different complaints and ailments and the lists of those found to be specially valuable have lengthened as their virtues have been proved.

The aromatic herbs, like mint and fennel, have a helpful effect for indigestion sufferers while garlic, chives, sage and rosemary are credited with disinfectant ability. Sage serves many purposes from that of making a good hair dye and, when dried and crumbled, an excellent tooth powder, to a rather pleasant tisane which, when cold, can also be used for gargling to help cure a sore throat. It is very noticeable now that interest in the medicinal uses of herbs has been revived and is increasing rapidly.

Two books on herbs are listed on p. 162.

COMPANION PLANTS

Plants that are helpful when planted close to others are called companion plants. Many of the aromatic herbs are useful in this way and there are other companion plants, like French marigolds, that give off root secretions which deter some persistent underground pests like eelworms.

It is interesting that gardeners have known for centuries that the presence of some plants seemed to be of benefit to others, but until recently were unable to find any explanation for this. Now it is beginning to be understood that the scent given off by such strong-smelling plants as garlic and onions, as well as by the fragrant herbs, is responsible. This acts as a repellent to unwanted insects. The old gardeners did, of course, understand that the scented herbs were helpful in attracting plenty of bees which pollinated the flowers of their fruit and vegetable plants. They also realised that some plants disliked growing near each other. Onions and members of the pea family are examples of this and, among the trees, oaks and walnuts.

In the old days there were several plants that were called 'plant doctors', as it was said that their presence increased the healthiness of a garden. Marigolds, chamomile and nasturtiums were thought to be of particular use in this respect.

Here are some examples of plants which seem to do well when grown near each other and which could be tried by children:
Onions, shallots, chives and sage help to keep carrots free from carrot fly. (But the later in the year carrots are sown, the less danger there is from carrot fly.)

Garlic should always be grown in rose beds, while parsley grows better when it is near roses.

Green chervil is helpful to the growth of radishes.

Mints are said to keep peas healthy although this may well be only an association of the delight of eating mint with fresh young peas.

Nasturtiums, trained up fruit trees, help to control woolly aphid pests and also help to keep black-fly off broad bean plants.

Thyme, hyssop and peppermint should be grown near members of the cabbage family to keep large white butterflies away.

FRUIT GROWING

The number and variety of different edible fruit plants that it is possible to grow in a garden depends on the amount of space and good light that is available.

Even a solitary standard apple, pear, plum or cherry tree takes up a lot of room, though one may be required to improve the garden landscape or for shelter purposes. Some varieties of these trees can be specially trained into a flatter shape, suitable for growing in thin hedge-form or against walls. Such trees, already trained, can be obtained from nurseries or garden centres. The exotic peaches, nectarines and apricots *can* be grown from stones but may need grafting (see p. 59) and, while they do best in greenhouses, can also be grown against protective walls with a south-, south-west or west-facing aspect. Fig trees also need protection. The fruit production of trees grown from seeds is uncertain and more reliable trees can be purchased from nurseries.

All fruit trees need careful manuring and pruning and must not be expected to produce a crop too early. For their first few years it is wiser to remove all but one or two of the young set fruits in case their development overtaxes the juvenile tree's strength.

Strawberries grow on herbaceous, leafy plants close to the ground and can produce a good crop during the first year. The other soft fruits—raspberries, currants, gooseberries, blackberries and loganberries—all grow on many-branched shrubs (called canes in the case of raspberries) and need careful yearly pruning. Blackberries and loganberries, which do well against walls, will need tying up.

To protect fruit and vegetables from birds which are hungry or have young to feed it may be necessary to grow the plants in netting cages. However, it is very important to make sure that the mesh is small enough to keep all the garden birds out, or the smallest may be trapped inside and instantly panic and injure themselves. The netting should always be completely taut, not sagging or having unfinished, overlapping folds or tucks at the bottom or corners: birds may be trapped in these, or even caught by the leg.

HOW LONG VEGETABLES AND SALAD PLANTS TAKE TO GROW OUTDOORS

VEGETABLE	PART EATEN	WHEN TO SOW OR PLANT OUT	APPROXIMATE TIME BETWEEN SOWING AND HARVESTING (WEEKS)
Asparagus pea	Whole unripe fruiting pods	Late April to early July	11–14
Bean, broad	Unripe seeds	November to March	15–26
Bean, French	Whole unripe fruiting pods	Late April to early July	11–14
Bean, runner	Whole unripe fruiting pods	Early May to June	11–15
Beetroot	Swollen roots	April to June	12–15
Brussels sprout	Leafy buds	Late March to May	24–30
Cabbage, spring green	Whole leafy crown	Early July to early September	30–36
Cabbage, winter (Savoy)	Whole leafy crown	Late March to May	19–25
Cabbage, red	Whole leafy crown	Late August to early October	35–45
Carrot	Swollen roots	Late March to early July	12–22
Cauliflower	Flower buds and young leaves	Late March to May	16–23
Corn salad or lambs lettuce	Green tops of young growing plants	Late March and repeat all summer	8–10
Courgette	Unripe seed-containing fruit	As soon as frost is past	14–19
Cress	Whole shoot	March until frosts	7–9 days
Garlic	Bulbs	March	24
Green chervil	Green tops of young growing plants	Late March and repeat all summer	10–12
Jerusalem artichoke	Root tubers	March to April after frosts	30–36
Landcress	Leaves	As soon as frost is past	8–14

VEGETABLE	PART EATEN	WHEN TO SOW OR PLANT OUT	APPROXIMATE TIME BETWEEN SOWING AND HARVESTING (WEEKS)
Lettuce	Leafy crowns	Nearly all year round under cloches. Late March in open	Depends on sowing time
Marrow	Unripe seed-containing fruit	As soon as frost is past	13–20
Melilot	Green tops of young growing plants	March	8–12
Mustard	Whole shoot	March until frosts	4–5 days
Onion (sets)	Basal bulb	February to April	13–20
Parsley	Leaves	Warm, spring weather	12–16
Parsnip	Swollen roots	Late February to April	29–32
Pea	Unripe seeds	Late March to early July	10–13
Potato	Root tubers	Late February to early May	14–18
Purple sprouting broccoli	Flower buds and young leaves	Late March to May	22–28
Radish	Swollen roots	March till frosts	3–6
Shallot	Basal bulb	February to April	13–18
Spinach (perpetual)	Leaves	March to July	12–16
Spring onion	Basal bulb and young leaves	Late February to July	12–14
Sunflower	Ripe seeds	April to May after frosts	30–32
Tomato	Ripe fruits	Strong young plants can be put out after frosts	22–34
Turnip	Swollen roots	March until frosts	10–12
	Leaves as winter greens	March until frosts	6–10

GARDENING NOTEBOOK

1. Start filling in the page for your vegetable planting diary. Remember to record the date, the name of the vegetable, the method of planting and the first sign of growth.

2. Make drawings of vegetable seeds. If possible grow a few of each in

damp conditions (see Fig. 30) so that you can watch their root and shoot development and draw these too, to illustrate your notebook.

3. Cut pictures of well-grown vegetables out of spare or old gardening catalogues and magazines. Mount these and add notes about growing methods, their history, country of origin and anything else of interest that you can find out about them.

4. Keep a note of the amounts of each crop harvested so that you will know what is worth growing in future years. Some cultivars grow better in different soils and in different parts of the country so if one is not successful try another one next year.

FURTHER TOPICS FOR DISCUSSION, OBSERVATION AND RESEARCH

1. Find out more about crop succession, or crop rotation as it is some-times called. Its history is interesting: the idea began in Suffolk, with a farmer who was known as 'Turnip' Townshend.

2. Herbs have been grown for cooking and flavouring as well as for medicines for centuries. Read more about them with special reference to their use as companion plants to other edible plants. Also find out some of the medicinal uses of the herbs you grow.

3. Vitamins, and their necessity to all forms of animal and plant life, are really only of fairly recent discovery. Try to find out more about them, about the vitamins our bodies need to keep us healthy and how we can obtain some of them from eating fresh fruit and vegetables.

6 · The flower garden

Most children, especially those with enquiring minds, will want to know the name of every plant in the garden. Every plant has a botanical name and many have common English names as well. There are many plants, however, particularly the less usual ones, that do not have common English names and so have to be known by their botanical names only. The English names in common usage often vary throughout the country and will not be understood in other countries. When for scientific reasons Latinised botanical names were evolved they began to be widely used by nurserymen and gardeners. It is important for young gardeners to understand how these names work before they can use them properly.

The popular naming of harebells gives a good example of how important these names can be. These plants are sometimes cultivated in rock gardens and also grow wild in the British Isles. They have as their botanical name *Campanula rotundifolia* and this stays the same wherever the plant is described or discussed. However, if we look at the common name, this plant is known as bluebell in Scotland and as harebell, blue bottle, heath bell, sheep bell, granny's tears or witches thimble in other parts of the country. To add confusion, these names may also be used to describe other plants in different parts of the country.

As these popular names are traditional, as well as often being very picturesque, they have occasionally been included. There is a list of several such names on p. 76, to which others can be added as children hear or read about them.

BOTANICAL NAMES

The system in use today of giving every plant two Latinised botanical names is due to the work of the Swedish botanist Carl Linnaeus in the eighteenth century. This is a very frivolous limerick about him, made up by a contemporary Canadian botanist:

> *There once was a chap called Linnaeus*
> *Who discovered all nature was chaos*
> *He set out to describe*
> *Every species and tribe*
> *So that chaos would no longer dismay us!*

Linnaeus spent his life travelling the world collecting and classifying plants. He arranged them into families according to their major botanical characteristics.

Harebells and Canterbury bells (*Campanula medium*), for example, belong to the bellflower family—*Campanulaceae*. All the members of this family have flowers made up of five petals joined together: the flowers are frequently bell-shaped. Plants such as chrysanthemums, daisies and marigolds have many small florets, often of two kinds, the inner, or disc-florets, and the outer, or ray-florets, all packed into compound or composite flower heads. These belong to the *Compositae* family. It is interesting for young people to start learning the different characteristics of botanical families: plants are often grouped into these in authoritative books about either wild or cultivated flowers.

Each family is split into genera (singular—genus) which are based on the plant's more-detailed botanical features. The family name is not used in the botanical name of the plant. Instead, the first name is that of the genus and always has a capital letter. The second name is, in most cases, applied to that plant only and is known as the specific or species name. Thus the botanical name of the common daisy is *Bellis perennis*, *Bellis* being the genus and *perennis* the species. The generic name is sometimes abbreviated to just its initial letter when it is clear to which genus reference is being made. Similarly, where several species of the same genus are listed two initial letters may be written. For example, several species of *Campanula* could be shown as *CC. medium, rotundifolia* and *isophylla*.

Some botanical names, like *Chrysanthemum, Camellia, Narcissus* and *Rhododendron* are easy for children to learn because they are in use all the time as common names and are already familiar. Other botanical names are easy, too, as the common names are so like the generic names. For example, roses belong to the genus *Rosa*, lilies to *Lilium* and primroses to *Primula*. It is worthwhile, though, even with the more difficult double botanical names, for young gardeners to make an effort to learn them when they encounter them as they are in such common usage. And, as mentioned, not all plants have common English names. Botanical names of plants in the text are usually included in brackets after the common English name.

All botanical names are printed in italics and have been derived from Latin or Greek, or are Latinised words from other sources. Some of them incorporate the names of famous botanists or the plant hunters who first found the plants. In other cases the plant may have been found years after the death of a person famous in the plant world and given his name as a commemorative gesture. Here are some examples of botanists and plant hunters who have had plants named after them:

LEONARD FUCHS (1501–1566), a respected botanist, had the genus *Fuchsia* named in his honour after it was found in America in 1645.

REVEREND ADAM BUDDLE (1660–1715), another botanist, is commemorated by having his name included in the popular *Buddleia davidii* or butterfly bush, which was not brought to this country until late in the nineteenth century.

PÈRE ARMAND DAVID (1826–1900), a French plant lover and explorer, shares *Buddleia davidii* with Adam Buddle and also has his name incorporated into *Clematis armandii*.

FRANK KINGDON-WARD, one of the most famous plant explorers of this century, who found and brought back many beautiful plants from the Far East (and also wrote about his journeys) has his name in *Rhododendron wardii*, among others.

REGINALD FARRER, another twentieth-century plant lover, gardener and plant collector, has had several plants named after him, including *Viburnum farreri*, as it is correctly named, although it is still sometimes known as *V. fragrans*.

Since Linnaeus first instituted the system, all known plants, all over the world, have each been given their own particular double international names by plant authorities. The initials or an abbreviated form of this authority's name is sometimes shown after the plant name, for example, holly, *Ilex aquifolium L*, or named by Linnaeus. Gardeners and plantsmen sometimes use only the first of the two botanical names when, perhaps, they do not know the second or specific half, or when talking in general terms. Then the plant is referred to as *Viburnum* sp, or a species in the genus *Viburnum*. Where several species are referred to this is written as *Viburnum* spp.

Hybrids are the result of interbreeding between two species. Their botanical names show this by having an × between the generic and specific names, for example the hybrid winter honeysuckle, *Lonicera × purpusii*. This was bred from *Lonicera fragrantissima* and *Lonicera standishii* and, as an established hybrid, has now been given a name of its own.

When plants of the same species interbreed naturally the offspring are usually known as varieties. When growers or nurserymen actually pollinate one species with another or select a particular plant that has special characteristics, the resulting offspring is called a cultivated variety or cultivar. The names of the varieties and cultivars are added on after the generic and species names. Varietal names are latinised as in *Buddleia davidii alba*, where *alba* is the variety. Cultivar names, which are selected by the grower, are shown as in *Buddleia davidii* 'Royal Red'. Sometimes cultivars are named in honour of well-known people, for example the rose 'Queen Elizabeth'.

POPULAR NAMES FOR SOME WILD AND GARDEN PLANTS

COMMON ENGLISH NAME	BOTANICAL NAME	POPULAR OR COUNTRY NAME (AND ORIGIN)
Autumn crocus (not a true crocus)	*Colchicum autumnale*	Naked ladies (Gloucestershire) Michaelmas crocus (Somerset)
Bee orchid	*Ophrys apifera*	Bumblebee (Surrey)
Common ivy	*Hedera helix*	Bentwood (Scotland and northern counties)
Cornflower (annual)	*Centaurea cyanus*	Bluebottle (Lincolnshire)
Daffodil	*Narcissus pseudonarcissus*	Lent lily Cuckoo's rose (Devon)
Golden rod	*Solidago canadensis*	Aaron's rod (this name is also used for mulleins)
Jacob's ladder	*Polemonium caeruleum*	Blue jacket (Northern Ireland)
Knapweed	*Centaurea nigra*	Hardheads
Lime tree	*Tilia europea*	Linden tree Whitewood tree (North Britain)
Monkey flower or musk	*Mimulus guttatus*	Gapmouth (Dorset)
Nettle	*Urtica dioica*	Naughty man's playthings (Sussex and other counties)
Periwinkle	*Vinca* spp	Blue Betsy (Oxford and other counties) Cut-finger
Rowan	*Sorbus aucuparia*	Mountain ash Whistlewood (Yorkshire)
Self-heal	*Prunella vulgaris*	Cut-finger Carpenters' herb
Sycamore	*Acer pseudoplatanus*	Locks and keys (Essex, Norfolk, Cambridgeshire)
Teasel	*Dipsacus fullonum*	Donkey thistles, hairbrushes, church broom (all from Somerset)
Violet	*Viola* spp	Cuckoo's shoes (Shropshire)
Wild clematis	*Clematis vitalba*	Old man's beard Grandfather's whiskers (Cornwall) Virgin's bower (Wiltshire and Hampshire)
Yew	*Taxus baccata*	Hampshire weed (New Forest) Poisonberry tree

GARDEN FLOWERS ALL THE YEAR ROUND

Everyone with a garden has the chance to create ever-changing patterns of colour throughout the year by choosing flowering plants carefully. The majority of flowers can be seen in the spring, summer and early autumn but it is possible to have a few flowers out even in the winter. A succession of flowers needs careful planning by young gardeners and it is necessary for them to find out which plants bloom at various times of the year. Sheltered corners will have to be used for the winter or pre-vernal (extremely early spring) flowers so that all-year-round colour can be obtained. When planning the flower garden a reminder should be given to include some plants that will attract bees and butterflies (see p. 32).

Bulbs

Spring bulbs, which include corms and tubers, should be planted in the previous autumn while they are dry and dormant. There is one exception to this rule as snowdrops are best moved when they are in full leaf or even in flower. Here are some suggested spring bulbs for children to grow, arranged in the order in which they usually flower:

winter aconite (*Eranthis hyemalis*); snowdrop (*Galanthus nivalis*); crocus (the species or named types flower earlier than the Dutch hybrids; try for *CC. aureus, tomasinianus* or *chrysanthus* hybrids); daffodils (*Narcissus* 'February Gold' and 'Peeping Tom' are two of the first to flower); bunch-flowered narcissus (e.g. *N.* 'Cragford' and, in protected places only, 'Soleil D'Or' and 'Paper White'); scilla (*Scilla sibirica*); several irises (*II. reticulata, danfordiae* and *histrioides* 'Major'); grape hyacinth (*Muscari armeniacum*); glory of the snow (*Chionodoxa luciliae*); late-flowering daffodils and narcissi (e.g. *NN.* 'Golden Harvest', 'Fortune' and pheasant's eye narcissus); hyacinths (*Hyacinthus* cultivars); tulips (*Tulipa* spp and cultivars).

N.B. The genus *Narcissus* covers plants commonly known as both daffodil and narcissus.

Other bulbs can be planted at various times in the spring and early summer to flower later in the summer and in frost-free autumns. Many of them are only half hardy and need to be lifted and kept in dry, warm shelter during the winter. These are some of the most attractive and easiest to grow:

anemones (*Anemone* spp); lilies (*Lilium auratum, canadense, candidum, henryi, pardalinum, regale, tigrinum*); ornamental onions (*Allium albopilosum, moly* and *siculum*); summer or cape hyacinth (*Galtonia candicans*); sword lilies (*Gladiolus* cultivars); tiger flower (*Tigridia pavonia*); tuberous begonia (*Begonia tuberhybrida*); turban flower (*Ranunculus asiaticus*).

True bulbs, corms and tubers are frequently classed together loosely and spoken of as bulbs or bulbous plants. Strictly speaking this is incorrect, although the three plant forms all demonstrate methods that have been adopted by the parent plants to ensure protection and good over-wintering conditions for next year's buds. Botanically, bulbs are buds enclosed in, and surrounded by, an accumulation of plant food which has been stored in the bases of old leaves. They divide and increase and the offsets thus produced are sometimes enclosed in the same outer, dry, scale cover. Corms are usually formed yearly, as new accumulations of plant food fill the swollen base of the old stem. They are often flat and rounded growths which are enclosed in a covering known as a tunic and the new buds form on top of them. Tubers are the swollen ends of underground shoots on which new buds will develop.

Annuals

These plants have to be sown from seed each year since the mature plants rarely withstand the winter. Because of this they have to complete their life cycles—growing, flowering, setting and dispersing seed—all in one season. The plant's ability to tolerate frosts and low temperatures determines when it should be sown or planted in the garden. Those which need some protection and should not be put outside until the risk of frost is past are called half-hardy annuals. Some hardy subjects can be planted out in the previous autumn to flower with some of the later spring bulbs.

The seeds of annuals which have not been collected should be allowed to disperse before the plants are removed in the autumn. In the following spring many of these seeds will grow and produce new plants. These are described as self-sown plants and their random distribution in the flower garden enhances an informal appearance.

Before choosing which annuals to grow, children should study seeds-men's catalogues to find out how high the plants become and what colour flowers they have. The half-hardy types should be avoided unless they can be sown in boxes first, keeping them protected until it is safe to plant out. The directions on the seed packet should always be read carefully before the seed is sown. Outside, flower seeds should be sown more haphazardly than vegetable seeds but it must be remembered that they still need adequate space between them. Here are a few suggestions of annuals for young people to try:

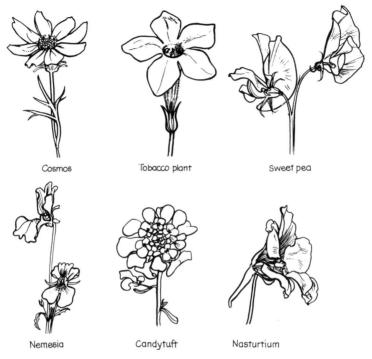

Cosmos   Tobacco plant   Sweet pea

Nemesia   Candytuft   Nasturtium

12. Six annual flowers

HARDY Californian poppy (*Eschscholtzia californica*); candytuft (*Iberis saxatilis*); English marigold (*Calendula officinalis*); larkspur (*Delphinium ajacis*); nasturtium (*Tropaeolum majus*); poached egg plant (*Limnanthes douglasii*).

HALF-HARDY baby blue eyes (*Nemophila menziesii*); Californian bluebell (*Phacelia campanularia*); Livingstone daisy (*Mesembryanthemum criniflorum*); nemesia (*Nemesia strumosa*); tobacco flower (*Nicotiana alata*); verbenas, or cherry pie (*Verbena* hybrids).

Some seedsmen sell packets of mixed seeds, especially selected for children, which can also be interesting to grow.

A wide range of bedding-out plants can be bought from nurserymen to provide colour in borders and tubs but they have to be chosen with care; they should not be bought too early in the season or if they already have a great many flowers. In the early spring polyanthus, large red and white daisies, huge-flowered pansies and many other beauties are displayed in shops but they can be disappointing if they have been brought out of their protection too early or brought on first with heat. If children are buying any of these plants they should choose healthy-looking, strong, young plants which have not yet come into full flower.

Biennials

These are the plants that take two years to produce flowers. Seed can be sown in the summer straight into the garden, or into boxes or cold frames, and the plants left to grow until the following spring. Many biennials produce a rosette of leaves, spread out into a ground-hugging, overlapping circle, which prevents other plants from growing too close. Young gardeners should make sure that they allow room for the leaf rosettes, if the plants have them, to lie flat in the boxes, and again when they are out in the garden.

Although these plants take some time to flower they are worth waiting for as they usually produce a colourful show and some will flower again in the following year. As with annuals, many biennials will produce self-sown plants but in some cases (for example, honesty) severe weeding is required to avoid invasion. Wallflower plants are sold in shops in the autumn and these will flower in the following spring, having been grown initially by the nurseryman. Here are some easily grown ones to try:

Canterbury bell (*Campanula medium*); evening primroses (*Oenothera* spp); forget-me-nots (*Myosotis* spp); foxgloves (*Digitalis* spp); hollyhock (*Althaea rosea*); honesty (*Lunaria annua*); mulleins (*Verbascum* spp); ornamental thistles; snapdragon (*Antirrhinum majus*); sweet William (*Dianthus barbatus*); wallflowers (*Cheiranthus* spp).

Perennials

These are plants that go on producing flowers year after year. In general they need little maintenance, except for staking and removing dead flower stems. Most perennials can initially be grown from seed or bought as small plants from nurseries. It may also be possible to obtain offshoots from friends' plants as described below. Perennials include many old favourites, such as:

blue anchusas (*Anchusa* spp); catmints (*Nepeta* spp); Christmas and Lenten roses (*Helleborus niger* and *orientalis*); columbine (*Aquilegia vulgaris*); leopardsbane (*Doronicum pardalanches*); lungwort (*Pulmonaria officinalis*); lupins (*Lupinus* spp and hybrids); Michaelmas daisy (*Aster novi-belgii*); New Zealand forget-me-not (*Brunnera macrophylla*); oriental poppy (*Papaver orientale*); phlox (*Phlox* spp); red hot pokers (*Kniphofia* spp).

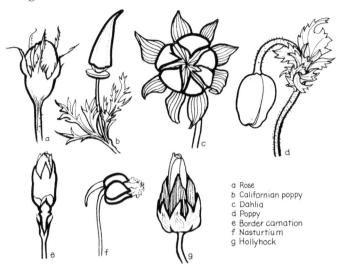

a Rose
b Californian poppy
c Dahlia
d Poppy
e Border carnation
f Nasturtium
g Hollyhock

13. *Variation in flower-bud shapes*

After a time perennials tend to grow into thick clumps which need to be divided into smaller plants. These should be lifted and divided as described in Chapter 4 but it is best to discard the central portion and replant only the outer pieces. These will be younger, more vigorous and less likely to have any pests and diseases.

Shrubs

These are the long-lived plants that grow from woody stems. They vary a great deal in height, spread and flowering and are useful in gardens because they do not need much attention. The wide range of shrubs and their uses is described in Chapter 9.

'Fun' plants

Encourage children to save a corner for a few amusing plants like the giant balsam (*Impatiens glandulifera*), also called policeman's helmet because of the shape of the back of the flowers. The bees love this and its handsome deep or pale

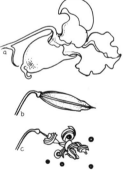

a Flower
b One whole flower
c Fruit exploding

14. *A 'fun' plant — policeman's helmet*

pink blossoms are succeeded by explosive seed pods which burst when they are ripe: they can be triggered off by passing people or animals. This seed dispersal mechanism helps to scatter the seeds well away from the parent plants. Occasionally specialist nurserymen offer seed of another plant with explosive fruits, the squirting cucumber (*Ecballium elaterium*) which has cucumber-shaped fruits growing near the ground. These send out a wet jet of slimy seeds if they are trodden on or touched when ripe.

Other 'fun' plants include some with weirdly-shaped flowers such as various *Asarum* and *Arisarum* spp. Mousetail (*Arisarum proboscideum*) is a low-growing perennial with small brown flowers that look like the hindquarters and tail of a mouse. *Aristolochia sipho*, known as Dutchman's pipe, is a climber with flowers like little Meerschaum pipes. Three shrubs with contorted twigs and branches are the contorted hazel (*Corylus avellana* 'Contorta'), also called the corkscrew hazel and Harry Lauder's walking stick tree, the Japanese willow (*Salix sachalinensis* 'Sekka') with curiously flattened, decurved stems and *Salix matsudana* 'Tortuosa'.

It can also be fun for children to look out for and grow plants of a familiar shape but with unusually-coloured flowers, like the blue pimpernel (*Anagallis linifolia* 'Monelii') and the white musk mallow (*Malva moschata*). Two really stinking-flowered plants, the dragon arum (*Dracunculus vulgaris*) with beautiful, huge flowers, and a pink crosswort (*Crucianella stylosa*) are both good for this section, but they should not be planted too near the house!

Plants for drying

Plants that can be picked and dried to save for making presents and winter flower arrangements will also be interesting to grow. These flowers should be picked when they are at their best and hung, stalks upwards, in bunches somewhere airy where they will not get over-hot or damp. Some of the plants that are particularly suitable for drying are called everlasting flowers or immortelles and are easy to grow. Children should look out for seeds of the various-coloured strawflowers (*Helichrysum* spp), Cupid's dart (*Catananche caerulea*), rosy daisy (*Acrolinium roseum*) and the green bells of Ireland (*Moluccella laevis*) as these all dry well. Other everlasting plants worth trying are:

Allium albopilosum; *Allium siculum*; bear's breeches (*Acanthus mollis*); Chinese lanterns (*Physalis* spp); giant carline thistle (*Carlina acaulis*); globe artichoke flowers (*Cynara* spp); globe thistle (*Echinops sphaerocephalus*); honesty (*Lunaria annua*); sea hollies (*Eryngium* spp); sea lavenders (*Statice* spp); straw daisy (*Helipterum monglesii*); *Xeranthemum annuum*; yarrows or maudlin plants (*Achillea* spp).

Ordinary cut flowers can also be dried to preserve the shape and colour of the blooms. This is done by using desiccants which draw all the moisture from the flowers, leaving them in a fragile and brittle state. These silica gel crystals are available from florists, supermarkets and garden centres and can be dried and used over and over again.

Ornamental grasses

a Common quaking grass
b Hare's-tail grass
c Hairy oat grass
d Ornamental brome
e Large quaking grass
f Foxtail grass
g Canary grass (on inside)
h Pony-tail grass (on outside)

15. A collection of ornamental grasses

Packets of mixed ornamental-grass seeds can produce an amazing assortment of intricately flower-spiked specimens. Many of them have very descriptive English names, and individual species can also be bought when young people have special favourites. If seeds are sown in late April or May, the grasses will flower in late summer. They can be picked, then dried or pressed and are very useful to add to summer flower arrangements, to use later when flowers are in short supply or to decorate various forms of handiwork.

Some of the ornamental grasses are exotics and their seeds are imported, so their flowers may look strange to us. Pampas grass (*Cortaderia argentea*) is a huge foreign grass but the ornamental-grass seed sold for the garden is usually from much smaller plants. A few grasses are grown for their coloured and variegated foliage rather than for their flowers. A kind of maize which has brilliantly striped green and cream leaves can be sown and is most decorative, although it needs plenty of space. The stiff, short tufts of near-blue leaves of the glaucous sheep's fescue (*Festuca glauca*) make neat little tussocks which can be eye-catching in the front of any flower border. Here are some ornamental grasses for which seeds can be obtained:

beard grass (*Polypogon monspeliensis*); blue meadow grass (*Koeleria glauca*); canary grass (*Phalaris canariensis*); cloud grass (*Agrostis nebulus*); feather grass (*Stipa pennata*); golden mist grass or Bowles' grass (*Milium effusum* 'Aureum'); hare's tail (*Lagurus ovatus*); Job's tears (*Coix lachryma jobi*); ornamental oats (*Avena sterilis*); ornamental wheat (*Triticum spelta*); ponytail grass (*Pennisetum longistylum*); quaking grass (*Briza maxima* and *minor*); rosy grass (*Tricholaena rosea*); squirrel's tail (*Hordeum jubatum*).

Ground-cover plants

These are so-called because they are usually low-growing and spread quickly to cover a large area of soil. They are particularly useful when planted between shrubs (see Chapter 9) as they prevent most of the weeds from growing, though careful weeding will be necessary until the plants become well established. Some of the best known are:

yellow archangel (*Lamium galeobdolon*); bugle (*Ajuga reptans*); creeping Jenny (*Lysimachia nummularia*); evergreen wood spurge (*Euphorbia robbiae*); ivies (*Hedera* spp); periwinkles (*Vinca* spp); rose of Sharon (*Hypericum* spp).

Climbing plants

Unsightly parts of the garden, such as walls, fences, sheds and garages, can be covered up by using climbing plants, as long as there is sufficient soil in which they can grow. They will all need to be tied to the support initially but, once established, some types of climbers that twine or have tendrils or hooked thorns will need no further help (see p. 92 for suggested kinds). If there are no suitable fences or walls, other supports, such as dead tree trunks or stumps, can be provided for climbing plants. Posts can be used for this purpose and even the clothes post could be camouflaged. Sometimes, usually in larger gardens, wooden frames and brick pillars are built for climbing plants, particularly roses, so that a covered walk, or a pergola, is produced. Other ideas can often be seen in public parks and large gardens.

ROCKERIES

A rockery in the garden makes an interesting feature and adds another dimension, as well as being a place for the young gardener to put a few of the low plants which, as opposed to the true alpines (see p. 96), grow on mountain slopes in the wild. The rocks are used to increase the illusion that this part of the garden represents, not a high mountain, but rather the foothills. Rock gardens should always look natural—as if a few rocks had tumbled down the slope. In warm parts of the country it is best to make the two main sides of the rockery face east and west so that none of the

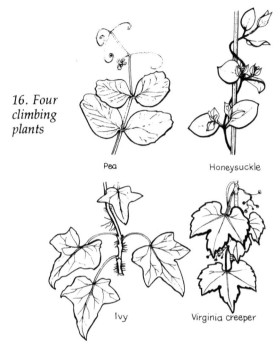

16. Four climbing plants

Pea

Honeysuckle

Ivy

Virginia creeper

plants suffer from exposure to too much sun. In colder climates the construction of north and south faces is preferable.

The site for the rockery should be in a sheltered part of the garden, as draughts of cold air are harmful to rock plants. They should be situated well away from trees so as to avoid their drip and leaf-fall. It is important to remember that all rock plants need good drainage and therefore most garden soils will be improved by the addition of some rough peat and possibly some gravel. A rough guide to the height for a rockery can be assessed if the level across 2·4–2·7 m (8–9 ft) of ground space never rises more than 60 cm (2 ft). In other words, the gradient should not be steeper than 1:4·5. The soil for the rockery should not be dug out of the surrounding area, which would leave a trench around it, but soil already dug out for the making of a garden pond (see Chapter 8) or other excavations could well be used. The soil should be patted down firmly while building up the mound and once it is high enough, the peak should be flattened to make a small plateau. The new hill should be left to weather for at least a week and, during this time, a child could carefully run up and over it several times to make sure that it is really firm.

It is always cheaper, and gives a more natural appearance, to use locally obtainable stone for the rocks, but it should not be flaky. Limestone, hard sandstone, tufa, granite and even roughly broken concrete can be used, although the last two are ugly before they are weathered and covered. Wide, flat-surfaced, slabby rocks should be avoided, as should any that are near spherical. The rocks should be positioned by digging out a place for each one and then filling in any spaces around them. Rock-moving is such heavy work that a system of leverage is helpful.

Many nurseries have rock-plant sections and there are famous specialists as well (see p. 165). Young gardeners should initially buy strong-looking plants, recommended as easy to grow, which promise to give good spreads of colour, and wait until later to specialise in those that are more difficult to grow. These are some strong and popular rock-garden plants:

aubrieta (*Aubrieta deltoidea*); dwarf campanulas (*Campanula* spp); dwarf phlox (*Phlox* spp); dwarf soapwort (*Saponaria ocymoides*); fairy foxglove (*Erinus alpinus*); mossy saxifrages (*Saxifraga* spp); rock rose (*Helianthemum nummularium*); rock pinks (*Dianthus* spp); thrift (*Armeria caespitosa*); viola (*Viola gracilis*).

A very attractive type of rock garden can be made on and in a low dry-stone wall. As the plants grow they will spill out in patches of colourful, natural falls and festoons. The construction of the wall will also provide an interesting project for children and plants should be put in pockets of soil in spaces between the stones.

PEAT-BLOCK GARDENS

These can be useful for cool, shady places and are excellent for plants like some ferns and small flowering species which dislike growing on chalk. They are ideally used on slightly sloping and north-facing sites. Direct south-facing positions should be avoided as the peat would dry out too quickly.

Peat blocks are sold by some garden centres and nurserymen. They are very light to move and put in place but before they are used they need a thorough soaking. The best place to soak them is in a rainwater butt, or tank, where they should be left for at least a couple of days. They should then be put out and left to drain before being placed in their final positions.

The bottom row of a peat-block wall should be set about 5 cm (2 in) into the ground and the subsequent rows should follow in the same way as bricklayers lay ordinary bricks, so that each one overlaps the joins between the two bricks below. Plants can be put in between the 'bricks' but the spaces must be filled with peat or lime-free soil. This in-filling should be tight and firm and should really be done before any planting takes place, then left for a week or two to set and weather. If tap water is hard and chlorinated it should not be used for watering the peat-block garden. Instead, soft water is safer and rainwater is best of all.

Rock-plant nurserymen will be able to advise on the range of plants that are particularly suitable for peat-block gardens but here are a few successful ones:

dwarf mint (*Mentha requienii*); dwarf rhododendrons (*Rhododendron* spp and cultivars); gentians (*Gentiana* spp); heaths and heathers (*Erica* and *Calluna* spp); may lily (*Maianthemum bifolium*); primulas (*Primula* spp); twin flower (*Linnaea borealis*).

GARDENING NOTEBOOK

1. Start filling in your flower planting diary, using a special coloured flower page with pictures (cut out or drawn) as a border, and record sowings, transplantings and the results you obtained.

2. Find and start cutting out pictures of plants and name them when they have been stuck in. Also start drawing flowers, looking very carefully at them and trying to match their colours if you paint them in. Look at the picture of the parts of the flower in Fig. 2 as you do this and try to recognise the various parts. Are the flowers spotted or all plain in colour? If only part of the flower is spotted, look at this carefully and see if it is an indication-path to visiting insects, so that they can find the way into the centre where any pollen and nectar are. Spots, patches of contrasting colours or, sometimes, grooved paths of this kind are known as honey or nectar guides. Draw flowers with honey or nectar guides and colour them in. Write a few notes on why you think these guides can be useful in helping pollination to take place.

3. Make an all-over brightly coloured picture of spring bulb flowers. It would be fun to use old bulb catalogues, if you have them, and cut out the pictures and stick them on.

4. Try to identify the insects that you see on flowers, make sketches when you can and add notes about what you think they are doing. When you know their names add them to the dated list of garden visitors (see p. 37).

5. Start a page of picturesque names for weeds, wild flowers and garden plants, similar to that on p. 76. Start with those that are mentioned throughout the book. These names are often plants' local and traditional names, and are interesting and fun to collect.

FURTHER TOPICS FOR DISCUSSION, OBSERVATION AND RESEARCH

1. Look carefully at flower buds. Many of them have green sepals covering them. Notice the texture, colour and joints where these sepals meet, as well as the shape of the buds. Try making a bud collage, cutting their shapes out of materials like velvet, silk or woolly cloth to match the texture of the bud coverings and then sticking them on (see Fig. 13 for some bud shapes).

2. Although most double flowers are not useful to bees and other pollen- or nectar-seeking insects, they are fascinating to examine carefully. Look at some closely and try to see how the petals are all packed in; some are in rows while others are in random positions. Try to draw some double flowers such as are shown on p. 32.

3. Look out for seeds on favourite plants after the flowers are over and collect some, making sure they are ripe; then keep them in separate labelled envelopes.

4. All grasses belong to a big family called *Graminae*. This includes cereal crops like maize, oats, wheat and barley as well as the many valuable grasses that provide edible grazing, or later hay, for our cattle, horses and ponies, and sheep. Others, including the huge pampas grass and various ornamental garden grasses have decorative flowers but a few grasses are obnoxious weeds (like couch grass and rough meadow grass). Look out for other wild grasses when they are in flower and collect and press them, as well as trying to name them (see p. 83).

5. Look out for plants (including trees) with separately sexed flowers (see p. 30), which may even grow on separate plants, as in the case with many of the hollies. Notice if the pollen from the male flowers is carried to the female flower by insects, or if it is blown there by the wind. Discuss variation in the ways of pollination. Several trees and shrubs which produce their flowers in cold weather, for example hazels (*Corylus avellana* and cultivars); the silk-tassel bush (*Garrya elliptica*); poplars and alders (*Populus* and *Alnus* spp), have male catkins from which pollen can be wafted about before insects are around to carry it.

6. Discuss colours and look out for brightly coloured flowers and then try to describe their colours without using the obvious word. For instance, do not always call scarlet geraniums 'red' or Himalayan poppies 'blue' but try

to think of a matching familiar object that gives the same image—perhaps pillar box for that blazing red and summer sky for that clear, pale blue. The Royal Horticultural Society sell a colour chart which is in some public libraries and is great fun to use. They have some interesting descriptions of colours and these can be matched to the petals and coloured leaves of some plants.

7. Look out for books about explorers and people who travelled over the world hunting for plants.

8. Try writing explanations of why you particularly like some of the flowers, trees and birds in the garden. Aim at making your words say exactly what you think.

7 · Outdoor container gardening

There is no need for young people to give up the idea of gardening if they have no garden, as nearly all plants—flowers, vegetables and fruit—can be grown satisfactorily in a wide range of containers. These can be kept on windowsills, in wall brackets or hanging in wire baskets or sisal slings, as well as being stood on the ground or raised on stands above it. Containers can also be both decorative and useful in gardens of all sizes. As much space as can be spared on balconies, porches and paved areas at home and at school should be used to accommodate growing plants.

In schools, different classes of children could specialise in different groups of container-grown plants. For example, older children might

17. *An outdoor container garden*

look after the larger plants like trees or fruit-producing shrubs. This would mean that there would need to be a scheme arranged in advance, so that the children would know that, for example, the top class in a junior school had reached the stage of looking after and studying the tree group. It would also add interest by giving a change in the kind of gardening undertaken at different stages in the young gardener's curriculum. Gardening Notebooks should be kept throughout the whole container-plant-growing study. Notes (and illustrations) should eventually have covered many different types of plants showing how they can be planted, looked after and placed to fill in space most efficiently and attractively. Descriptions of their habit, which may be creeping, upright, twining, climbing, scrambling or drooping and pendulous, should be included.

An enormous number of assorted containers can be used; the only limitation is that they must be sound and strong enough to hold the weight of soil that is necessary to fill them. They can be wooden boxes, tubs, tins of various sizes and shapes, old sinks or baths, metal or plastic bowls, pans or buckets. They may not look beautiful, but this will not affect the plants' growth and, if they are carefully arranged, most of them will be hidden by the plants as they grow. If preferred, some of the wide range of special plant containers can be bought for the purpose. The plastic ones are particularly useful as they are lighter and easier for children to move around. All these containers must have adequate drainage, in the form of holes at the bottom, so that any surplus water can drain away. They must also have room for enough depth of soil. This means from a minimum depth of 23 cm (9 in) for small plants and up to 60 cm (2 ft) or more for bigger, longer-living plants.

Growing bags, which are obtainable from garden centres, stores and some nurseries, are often useful here. They are made from heavy-duty polythene and are already filled with special composts based on peat or shredded bark. Seeds or plants are inserted through an aperture (indicated on the top and cut out at home) and subsequently kept watered as they grow.

Containers placed on the floor should have level props, such as bricks, underneath them so that they are not sitting in a puddle after a shower of rain. They should all be arranged in their final positions while they are empty (apart from the small, hanging containers) as they may be too heavy to move once they have been filled with soil.

Garden tools for the young container gardener can be very simple. The following are all useful: small hand fork and trowel, light watering can with detachable rose spray, pair of strong kitchen scissors, and old kitchen knives, forks and spoons which are particularly useful when moving small plants or dealing with small containers.

CHOOSING THE PLANTS

The aspect of the growing space, or the direction which it faces, will govern the amount of sun and shade in the container area and hence which plants can be grown. Almost all plants enjoy some sun. A few, like cacti and succulents, can survive in full, hot sun all day while others prefer some shade. The nurseryman will be able to advise on the best plants to grow when he knows the aspect. As in all gardens it is wisest to plant the plants which will grow tallest at the back where they will not overshadow the smaller ones. The competition for light goes on all the time, wherever plants grow, and getting enough light is a matter of life or death to them.

The young gardener should try to visit several well-established container-plant gardens and nurseries (refer to lists of gardens open to the public on p. 127, local directories and newspapers, and enquire about others from gardening friends) before buying any plants or even seeds. Careful notice should be taken of the way in which all the space is used and also of particular plants, such as leafy types and others like ferns (see p. 94), which will grow in less-promising situations than flowering plants. The plants chosen must suit the available containers. For example, it is no good buying a standard tree unless a deep tub can be provided for it. Children should be encouraged to buy only a few plants at first to arrange in the container space available, otherwise overcrowding and disappointment will result.

PLANTS FOR SUNNY PLACES

Depending on the height of the immediate surroundings, any spaces available for container plants, if facing south, east or west, will have some sun during the day and so will be able to support a wide range of flowers, fruits and vegetables. Some will need a wall or fence for support and so occupy little space, others are particularly suited to growing in hanging baskets and windowboxes, while the rest can be cultivated in various containers on the ground.

1. Against walls

FLOWERING AND FOLIAGE PLANTS of twining and scrambling habit *Clematis montana* and other spp; climbing roses (e.g. 'Ena Harkness', 'Albertine'); cup and saucer plant (*Cobaea scandens*); honeysuckles (*Lonicera periclymenum* and others); ivies (*Hedera helix* and others); morning glory (*Ipomaea tricolor*); passion flower (*Passiflora caerulea*);

summer and winter jasmines (*Jasminum officinale* and *nudiflorum*); Virginia creeper (*Parthenocissus quinquefolia*).

VEGETABLES pea ('Recette', 'Kelvedon Wonder' or 'Little Marvel'); runner bean ('Gina' or 'Goliath'); tomatoes in deep containers (also tamarindo tree tomatoes (*Cyphomandra betacea*), sometimes called tamarillas, from Saracen Truth Seeds; see p. 165).

FRUIT cultivated blackberry ('Bedford Giant', 'Himalayan' or 'Denver Thornless'); loganberry; raspberry ('Lloyd George' or, for autumn fruiting, 'September'); strawberry, which can be grown vertically in special polythene tubes, such as those in tower pots from Ken Muir (see p. 165) ('Grandee', 'Dormanil', 'Tamella', 'Pantagruella', 'Gento', 'Rabunda'); specially trained apple and other fruit trees (see p. 69).

18. *An attractively planted windowbox*

2. In hanging baskets or wall-mounted containers

These should be bought with a drip-tray or should be lined with polythene to stop water leaking from them. A light, mossy peat compost or John Innes No 2 or 3 should be used.

FLOWERING AND FOLIAGE PLANTS of drooping habit bellflowers (*Campanula isophylla* and *poscharskyana*); some cacti and succulents in the summer only, for example, rat-tail cactus (*Aporocactus flagelliformis*) and string of beads cactus (*Senecio rouleyanus*); canary creeper (*Tropaeolum peregrinum*); *Fuchsia* spp and hybrids; ivy-leaved geranium (*Pelargonium peltatum*); lobelia (*Lobelia erinus*); nasturtium (*Tropaeolum majus*); *Tradescantia* spp; *Zebrina* spp.

VEGETABLES   tomato 'Sub-Arctic Cherry'.

3. In containers on the ground

FLOWERING PLANTS   Virtually all flowering plants can be grown in containers—annuals, herbaceous plants and bulbs (see Chapter 6), and trees and shrubs (see Chapter 9).

VEGETABLES   Most types can be grown in containers as long as they are not giants. Particularly suitable are: dwarf French bean ('Limelight', 'Rainier'); garlic; lettuce ('Little Gem', 'Tom Thumb'); potato (one tuber to a large, bucket-shaped container); radish ('Red Prince', 'Icicle'); shallot ('Dutch Yellow'); spinach ('Cleanleaf'); spring onion ('White Lisbon'); sweet pepper ('Canape') needs frost-free, sunny, sheltered place; tomatoes (dwarf cultivars, such as 'Tiny Tim', 'Pixie').

HERBS   chives; marjoram; mint (in a container to itself); parsley; sage; thyme; winter and summer savories.

FRUIT   Many types of fruit tree can be grown in deep containers. They must have adequate depth and moisture to prevent them drying out and the container should be at least 90 cm (3 ft) in diameter. Staking, or careful tying to a wall or other support, will be needed at first. The following can be grown in containers although the actual choice of cultivar depends on the situation of the containers (see p. 90): apple (the dwarf kinds are worth looking out for); fig; peach; pear; plum. Alpine strawberries such as 'Alexandria' can also be grown, in tubs with holed sides.

PLANTS FOR SHADED PLACES

Although some flowering plants, such as the exotic camellias and the rose 'Mermaid', can tolerate a large proportion of shade, it is, on the whole, the leafy plants without showy flowers that do best without much sun. It is not necessary to despair, though, if the only space available is virtually always in the shade. Ornamental ivies and some evergreen trees, like box, holly, Irish yew and dwarf conifers grow well. So do the all-green ferns and ground creepers such as Irish moss or mind-your-own-business (*Helxine soleirolii*) which can survive without any sun at all.

   Encourage young gardeners to try for some dramatic effects on walls. They could use rapid-growing climbers, like the Russian vine (*Polygonum baldschuanicum*), and also trailing-stemmed plants springing from containers on wall brackets. They can find plenty of ideas for plants to grow by looking in parks and gardens to see which ones flourish in the shade. Ground containers should be carefully arranged to give a massed green effect at different levels and small pots can be used between the bigger boxes and troughs. Plants with drooping stems should be grown at the sides of the bigger containers so that they hide the sides and sharp edges. Both shiny and matt-leaved plants should be used and one should always ask for shade-tolerant plants when buying any from nurseries and garden centres.

A mirror on one or more shady walls could be tried, framed in climbing plants, so that the illusion of a garden twice the size is created by the reflection. Any wall tops to which there is access can be improved by fixing soil-holding containers to them for trailing or pendulous plants, together with some upright ones. Window and door surrounds can also be made more exciting by plants that produce long growing shoots.

Children can use their imagination to make shady grottoes (see p. 124), making a foundation of stands of different heights, on which containers can be arranged to provide soil. A fernery, using hardy species like hartstongue (*Phyllitis scolopendrium*), common polypody (*Polypodium vulgare*), the lady fern (*Athyrium filix-femina*) and the male fern (*Dryopteris filix-mas*) can be cultivated and different kinds of ferns collected in order to enjoy the varying shapes of their green fronds.

PLANTING THE CONTAINERS

Most containers, particularly the deeper ones, take more soil to fill them than one would imagine. Soil is usually expensive to buy, so take advantage where possible of friends with gardens who may be willing to supply some. Each container will need a 5 cm (2 in) drainage layer at the bottom which can be made from brick chips, pebbles or fragments of broken tiles or pots. The soil will be improved if some peat is mixed with it to increase the humus content and a little sharp sand added to help the drainage. The container should be filled half-full or, if necessary, two-thirds full, with this garden soil mixture, then topped-up to within 1 cm ($\frac{1}{2}$ in) of the rim with as good a potting compost as can be afforded (see pp. 42 and 98). Peat should not be used by itself for filling any but very shallow containers as it is too light when used alone to provide firm anchorage for growing roots. It also dries out easily and is very difficult to re-wet.

The soil should be allowed to stand and settle for at least a week, the surface being firmed repeatedly with the flat of the hand and the soil being kept damp by watering gently. The seedlings or bought plants should be planted into the containers as though they were being put into an ordinary garden, preparing the hole, allowing the roots to spread and then filling in carefully and re-firming the surface.

If possible the plants should be looked at every day to make sure that they are not too dry though the containers should not be overwatered, nor given water when the sun is shining on them. Container-grown plants will need more feeding than those out in the garden, as watering and heavy rainfalls are inclined to wash the soil nutrients through more quickly. These therefore need renewing. Children should be advised to avoid buying artificial, inorganic or chemical fertilisers and should ask instead for those made from natural or organic materials. The directions on how to apply these fertilisers should be read very carefully and they should be used only as recommended. Applying liquid fertilisers directly on to the leaves (foliar feeding) could also be useful in these circumstances.

Holidays, particularly from school, may provide problems of long periods of virtual neglect of the growing plants. It would be a good idea if neighbours could water them while their owners are away and if specially organised teams of young gardeners could visit school gardens in order to keep an eye on the plants and water them regularly.

MINIATURE ROCK OR ALPINE GARDENS

Plants that grow in high, mountainous places are known as alpines. Some gardeners find their way of growth and their shapes very fascinating and, as many of them can be grown successfully in rock gardens here in Britain, there is an Alpine Garden Society, with a junior branch, for growers of all ages to join (see p. 166). It is not necessary to have a big

Sempervivum tectorum
(rosette form)

Douglasia laevigata
(cushion form)

Cyclamen neapolitanum
(eventually forms a leafy mat)

19. Three alpine plants

garden to grow alpines. They can be cultivated in a much smaller way, out of doors, in raised containers such as old sinks and troughs or straight into tufa rock (see p. 99).

Alpines are used to hard conditions in their natural surroundings. The different ways in which they grow, often in small, compact forms, like rosettes, buns or cushions, as well as in low, ground-hugging mats, help them to hang on and survive the strong winds and long periods of drought which they have to face on the exposed mountain sides. Many of these plants are, in their natural surroundings, covered by snow all through the winter. When it melts, their roots have a good flow-past of water; this suits them as alpines do not like permanently wet ground. So, one of the more important things to remember when growing alpines is the necessity for good drainage.

All plants need moisture to keep them alive but where alpines grow wild there may be only occasional rainfalls after the snow has melted. They have, therefore, become adapted to conserve moisture so that they do not dry out.

A plant's ordinary way of giving off moisture, in the form of water vapour, is through the small holes, or pores, on the upper and lower surfaces of its leaves. This process is called transpiration. Plants which grow in places where the weather conditions make it difficult for their roots to obtain a regular supply of moisture (see also cacti and succulents, p. 135), or which are exposed to great heat or strong, drying winds, have various methods of preventing the loss of too much water vapour through their leaf surfaces. Some have small, thick-skinned leaves. Others have narrow, almost needle-shaped leaves with in-rolled margins or edges, or, if their leaves are wider, their surfaces may be covered by a mat of thick hairs, or even spines. All these are ways of preventing water vapour evaporating from the leaves as fast as it would from plants with bigger, smoother-surfaced, thin-skinned leaves. Other alpines, such as stone-crops (*Sedum* spp), store moisture in fat, fleshy, small leaves.

Choice of container

It is important to find a suitable, strong and attractive container in which to make a miniature rock garden, as once it is laid out it can last for many years. The young gardener should look out for old-fashioned china sinks in builders' yards, as these can be made into excellent containers. If their sides are too shiny and unnatural-looking, they can be scored with a screwdriver and then covered with a bonding agent, obtainable from a paint shop, before being coated with a mixture of cement, sharp sand and fine peat. This treatment makes the sink look like an old stone one which would be expensive to buy these days. The Alpine Garden Society (see p. 163) supply an excellent book called *The Handbook of Rock Gardening*, edited by R. C. Elliott, which contains instructions for making a sink for such a garden.

There are also plenty of plastic, sink- or trough-shaped containers available. Some look better and more like natural stone than others but, whichever type is chosen, it is essential that it should have drainage

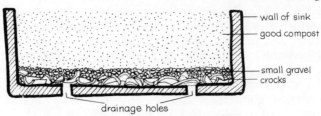

wall of sink
good compost
small gravel
crocks
drainage holes

20. How to fill a sink

holes, or possibly only one, such as the plughole in the case of an old sink.

As with other containers, the sink should be set in position before it is filled with soil. Two supports, brick ones are good, should bring the container to the most convenient height for working. One support should be slightly lower (about 1 cm (½ in)) than the other and the drainage hole should be placed at this end. The best way to fill the container so that it is ready for planting is shown in the diagram. When full it should be allowed to stand for a week or so to allow it to settle. The surface of the compost should be pressed down firmly, both at first and again whenever it has to be disturbed for planting.

Landscaping

When designing their miniature rock gardens, children should look out for ideas from other, already-planted ones. Some nurseries specialise in alpine plants and are ready to advise about those that are best to try (see p. 165). Garden centres may have examples of nicely landscaped sinks. Even pictures in a book may give them some guidance. Many of the gardens use a rock or two and perhaps a dwarf tree to add interest and height. Tufa rock is light and easy to handle (see p. 99) in comparison with other rocks and small pieces of it can be put in position before any plants are inserted. The rocks must be well set into the earth and not just perched on the surface.

Some plants are bound to spread profusely once they are established so the number put in initially should be limited. Otherwise the selection of what to grow is a matter of individual choice. Here are some alpine plants to choose from (plants marked * can be used at the sides and corners of the container so that, as they grow, they can hang over the edges):

CUSHION OR BUN-SHAPED   alpine pink (*Dianthus alpinus*); *Douglasia laevigata*; Kabschia saxifrages (*Saxifraga* spp); moss campion (*Silene acaulis*); pearlwort (*Sagina glabra*); primulas, including *Primula juliana*

'White Cushion'; rock jasmine (*Androsace sarmentosa*); thrifts (*Armeria caespitosa* and cultivars); yellow whitlow grass (*Draba aizoides*).

MAT-FORMING SPREADERS bellflowers* (*Campanula poscharskyana* and *portenschlagiana*); blue-flowered shamrock (*Parochetus communis*); Corsican mint (*Mentha requienii*); gentians (in acid soils only) (*Gentiana acaulis* and *sino-ornata*); houseleeks (*Sempervivum* spp); rock pansy (*Viola cornuta*); rock phlox* (*Phlox subulata* and cultivars); rock soapwort* (*Saponaria ocymoides*); rock yarrows (*Achillea* spp); sandwort (*Arenaria balearica*); stonecrops (*Sedum* spp); thymes* (*Thymus* spp).

BULBS crocus (*Crocus chrysanthus* hybrids, *biflorus* and *laevigatus*); glory of the snow (*Chionodoxa lucilae*); miniature irises (*II. danfordiae, histrioides* and *reticulata*); miniature narcissi (*NN. bulbocodium, cyclamineus* and *asturiensis*); miniature tulips (*Tulipa edulia, humulis* and *tarda*); scilla (*Scilla sibirica*); snowdrops (*Galanthus nivalis,* plus other spp and cultivars).

SHRUBS coral bush (*Helichrysum corallioides*), needs frost protection; garland flowers (*Daphne* spp); heaths and heathers (*Calluna* and *Erica* spp); rock roses* (*Helianthemum* spp and cultivars).

TREES dwarf false cypresses (*Chamaecyparis pisifera* and *obtusa* 'Intermedia'); Noah's ark tree (*Juniperus communis* 'Compressa').

When planting the miniature garden the young grower should try to work from a prepared, drawn plan, knowing exactly where each plant is to go. A small hole should be dug for each one so that the roots have enough room, and then the plants should be covered in carefully and firmly. When, later on, other plants are being added, the older ones should not be disturbed. The old kitchen fork and spoon come in useful here as miniature garden tools. The plants should be watered in well.

A ROCK GARDEN WITHOUT A STONE CONTAINER

An attractive rock garden for alpines can be made from a chunk of tufa rock. The size of the chunk will depend on the space available and the cost of this light, porous rock, which can be expensive. It is only quarried in a few areas, such as Derbyshire and Wales, which are rich in mineral springs and, unless local firms are found, its cost rises. It

21. A tufa rock garden

can be bought from rock-garden specialists but unfortunately it is never cheap.

The rock should be stood on earth or on a waterproof tray. It must be kept damp, then the plants will grow from holes in the sides and top if they are planted in carefully. The holes should be drilled at a slightly downward angle, wide enough to suit the plants' roots and about 7·5 cm (3 in) deep. They should be half-filled with a good potting compost and the roots inserted carefully. The rest of the hole can then be filled in with compost, making sure that the plant is firm and that the filling is flush with the surface of the rock. Again, it is important not to overcrowd this kind of rock garden until it can be seen how vigorously the plants are growing.

MODEL GARDENS

Children can obtain a great deal of pleasure and interest by designing and making a miniature garden, using dwarf forms or species of colourfully flowered plants in sinks or tubs (see plants suggested for rock gardens on p. 86). Small beds can be laid out and paths put down, as well as real ponds (by using polythene or foil containers or old dishes). Grass seed can be sown and 'mowed' as it grows with scissors.

It is surprising how many suitable tiny plants can be found. They include saxifrages (*Saxifraga* spp), dwarf sandwort (*Arenaria balearica*) and several prostrate toadflaxes (*Linaria* spp). It is entertaining looking out for them and children seem particularly good at spotting minute flowers in all kinds of different gardens. Midget forms of bedding-out plants can also be used, as well as dwarf shrubs and trees.

The whole idea could be made into a group project, using deep, waterproof trays, to landscape a model village and then plant out the gardens of the cottages, the manor house and any open spaces.

It is also possible to make a small water garden in a wide, shallow container (see p. 145), using the smallest aquatic plants.

GARDENING NOTEBOOK

1. Start a diary page for container planting, arranging the suitable headings in the way described on p. 60).
2. Collect pictures, and make notes under them, of the plants that you grow. Try too, to illustrate this notebook with some photographs of your balconies, school yards or patios when the plants are at their best.

3. When you grow vegetables in containers, keep records of the amounts that are harvested, so that you know what is worth growing in other years, as well as which ones particularly suited your conditions.

4. Keep lists of plants that you see in other people's container-growing places. Always ask for the plants' exact names so that you can order seed another season.

5. Look out for alpine plants and notice the ways in which they grow. There are some pictures on p. 96. Try to make drawings to illustrate others that you see and add your own comments about their various methods of growing and how you think they hinder moisture loss.

FURTHER TOPICS FOR DISCUSSION, OBSERVATION AND RESEARCH

1. Discuss the ways in which climbing plants manage to pull themselves up into the light, and try to find out more about them. Notice particularly which way runner beans or the bindweeds (*Convolvulus* spp) twine round their supports. If you untwine them gently and then wind them up in the opposite direction, will they stay like this? Look out for plants with tendrils. Can you find any surfaces that Virginia creeper (*Parthenocissus quinquefolia*) cannot cling to?

2. Visit if you can a specialist alpine nursery and look at the great number of different plants. Reginald Farrer, a great garden enthusiast who loved mountains and their plants, wrote about them in his most famous book *The Rock Garden*, and in others, and some of his descriptions are delightful to read. It would be interesting to discover the names of other mountain-exploring plant lovers.

3. There are a few alpine plants growing wild in North Wales and in Scotland. The Nature Conservancy Council (see p. 166) will supply information about nature reserves where British alpines might be seen: most of them are very rare and must never be picked but they are fun to find so that their surroundings can be observed.

8 · The garden pond

Children can gain a great deal of fun and interest from a garden pond, both during its construction and afterwards. On an aesthetic level the pond will add greatly to the beauty of the garden.

The construction of a pond is a relatively large project but one with which children can be fully involved, though some of the construction work may be too heavy for them to manage on their own. The pond's shape and position have to be decided upon, and then plants and fish, if wanted, have to be chosen for it. Once the pond has become an established feature of the garden it should start attracting many different kinds of wildlife for the children to observe.

It is far easier to make a small garden pond now that waterproof linings can be obtained in the form of butyl rubber sheeting and moulded polythene. These cut out the worst of the work which used to lie in putting down the concrete liner. The site for the pond should be discussed carefully. It should be well clear of trees as falling leaves will soon clog it and cause problems as they decay. It should also be in a light place but not one which is exposed to the sun all day long. The pond should be constructed on level ground unless any slopes can be corrected without too much extra work. Like everything else, the size of the pond will depend on the room available but the larger it is, the greater the interest it will arouse in terms of the numbers of creatures and plants it will accommodate. There are usually many places in the garden which are suitable for a pool. An informal-shaped pool can be placed in the lawn as a feature in its own right or to add further interest at the base of a rockery (see p. 84). A formal pool with straight edges could be placed in a patio or other paved area but could prove to be a trap for some forms of wildlife unless they are provided with a shallow sloping exit.

PREPARATIONS

Once the site for the pool has been decided upon, the length and width of the space available should be measured. Children can then draw some sketch plans of pools which will fit into this space, remembering to allow a clear 30 cm (1 ft) all round so that there will be a level edge. Apart from this the shape of the pool is largely a matter of their personal taste but the warning should be given that the more complicated the design the harder it will be to construct. Corners should be avoided as they make a pond very difficult to clean out.

The depth of the pond will govern the choice of plants to be grown in it. Some of the larger plants, water lilies, for example, will need a depth of 45–60 cm (1½–2 ft) while marginal plants will be best placed on a shelf constructed round the edge 7·5–10 cm (3–4 in) below the surface of the water. The pond must have one very shallow end, with a long, gradual slope so that birds and any visiting mammals, like hedgehogs, can drink from it safely. The shallow slope is necessary, too, to allow the amphibians—frogs, toads and newts—to climb in and out of the pond. The other sides should be fairly steep.

When purchasing the lining material it would be best for young gardeners to take their sketch plans to the garden centre or shop for advice. If

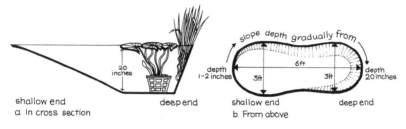

22. *A garden pond showing deep and shallow ends*

a butyl rubber sheet is to be used they should make sure that its width and length are those of the pond plus twice the depth at its deepest part. A moulded polythene liner should only be bought if there is one similar to the sketch, with one long, shallow, sloping edge.

CONSTRUCTING THE POND

Before digging begins children should mark out the outline of the pond with pegs or coloured twine or tape stapled to the ground. They will probably need help in digging out the soil to excavate a hole the shape and depth of the pond. It is best to start digging at the deepest part and from there move first to one end and then the other. They should not put the soil which is removed right at the edge of the hole as the liner will have to be laid there. If they are going on to construct a rockery (see p. 85) they can use the spare soil for this.

When the hole has been dug out to the measurements on the plan, they should tread down the bottom and pat the sides so that they are firm, being careful to remove all stones, or anything else that might tear the liner. The surface should be as smooth and neat as possible and it is sometimes a good idea to sift in a thin layer of sand or fine soil to cover up any irregularities.

If a moulded polythene liner is being used it can be put in position at this stage, while the butyl rubber sheet should be spread out, making sure that the centre of the sheet is over the centre of the hole. Bricks or large flat stones should be spaced evenly all the way round the edge to hold it down.

The centre of the sheet can then be gently filled with water, the butyl rubber stretching to dip down into the shape of the hole. Ordinary polythene will not do this as it is not sufficiently elastic. It will not matter if, as it is being filled, the edges of the sheet are at first slightly drawn in and begin wrinkling. When the new pond is full, the edges of the sheeting, if too wide, can be trimmed back to 15 cm (6 in). If the flap is still very wrinkled it can be nicked at the outside edge to make it lie flatter, but in any case it will be covered up and so will not show.

There are two possible ways of covering the edges of the liner. Stone slabs or crazy paving can be laid all round the pond, on top of the sheet, the spaces between them being packed with soil rather than cement. Then small plants like creeping thyme (*Thymus serpyllum*), Corsican mint (*Mentha requienii*) or other small flowering rock plants (see pp. 98–99) can be inserted there. The edging stones must be so close to the edge of the water that they are almost overhanging. If the pond is being constructed in the lawn a grass edging may look more attractive. In this case, the turf should be carefully peeled back and the liner laid underneath it.

The water in the new pond should be left to settle for a week or so, particularly if rainwater has not been used, so that it ripens or matures. If a fine green scum appears on the surface of the pond, do not worry as this will disappear when the water plants are put in and begin to grow.

PLANTS

The plants used in and around the edges of the pond will contribute greatly to its overall appearance and interest so children should try to landscape it carefully, making drawings of how it should look. Types of plants suitable for growing in and around a pond fall roughly into three categories and they should look out for these in other people's gardens, or water-garden centres if they visit them.

1. ROUND THE EDGE Some plants grow well with their roots perma-

nently wet and so thrive close to the edges of ponds, lakes and streams. These are known as marginal plants.

2. IN THE WATER   Other aquatic plants have their roots in the soil or mud at the bottom of the water of natural ponds, or in containers in lined ponds. They help to keep the water fresh as their leafy branches grow through it, giving off oxygen, and are called oxygenating plants. Some of these, such as water lilies, are known as surface-flowering plants, as they have flowers that emerge above the surface. The leaves of water lilies float on the surface but their roots must be anchored.

3. ON THE WATER   There are also plants that float on the surface of the water with their roots dangling and unanchored. These are the floaters and they can only survive where the water is still.

When choosing suitable plants children should look through the list from an aquatic-plant grower, making sure that they pick out hardy plants and not those that will die as soon as there is a frost. The ultimate size of the plant is also important and young plants should be spaced out accordingly. Putting in too many plants initially will only mean that some will have to be removed later.

No loose soil should be put into lined ponds. Instead it is wiser to plant the marginal and oxygenating plants in special water-plant containers. These are usually made from plastic and have holes punched in their sides. Before they are filled with soil and the plants put in, they should be lined with sacking to prevent the soil seeping out.

A little gravel may be scattered over the butyl sheeting to make the pond bottom look more natural and a few short-stemmed plants, such as

Shallow end   Deep end

23. A garden pond with established plants

water forget-me-nots and watercress, can be grown from stem cuttings (see p. 56). They should be tucked under the gravel at the shallow end and will soon put out roots.

Here are some suggestions for different plants that could be selected to grow in and around the pond:

1. MARGINAL PLANTS FOR EDGING
Tall: arrowhead (*Sagittaria sagittifolia*); reed mace or lesser bulrush (*Typha minima*); water plantain (*Alisma plantago-aquatica*); yellow flag or iris (*Iris pseudacorus*).
Shorter: marsh marigold or kingcup (*Caltha palustris*); monkey musk (*Mimulus guttatus*); pond spike rush (*Eleocharis palustris*).
2. OXYGENATING PLANTS broad-leaved pondweed (*Potamogeton natans*); hornwort (*Ceratophyllum demersum*); starworts (*Callictriche* spp); water milfoil (*Myriophyllum spicatum*); water lilies (*Nymphaea* spp).
3. FLOATERS Frogbit (*Hydrocharis morsus-ranae*); water fern or fairy moss (*Azolla caroliniana*) (slightly tender); water hawthorn (*Aponogeton distachyus*).

Do not encourage the growing of duckweeds in any but miniature ponds (see p. 108); they tend to increase too fast and cover the whole surface of the pond, but in a tiny area they can be controlled. If it is only a small pond not more than one water lily should be planted as it will soon become overcrowded. Children should study the lists to find the more-compact-growing forms.

FISH

Fish need shelter and plenty of cover, so must not be put into the pond until the plants have sweetened the water and have grown enough to make good shade for them. Then start with a few goldfish.

Experienced pond-keepers say that the fancy breeds of fish, although they may look attractive in indoor tanks and aquaria, are far too delicate for outdoor ponds and will only die if they are tried. They also emphasise that wild fish, or any that have been caught in country ponds or streams, must not be taken home to be introduced into garden ponds that already have fish in them. Apart from the fact that they might introduce fish diseases, they are far too used to fighting for their lives and would quickly kill off any goldfish. Also, the space restriction and other conditions would not suit them, so it is best to leave them where they are.

A fish supplier can advise on how many fish a pond can support but a rough guide is that at least 62 sq cm (10 sq in) is needed for every centimetre of fish length.

Fish should not need much feeding in outdoor ponds as long as they have adequate space and plenty of aquatic plants. If they are fed at all, properly blended fish food should be bought from a pet shop. Care must be taken that none is left floating on the water surface; it will only cause pollution as it decays. The food should always be scattered on to the same part of the surface each day and any surplus scooped off after the fish have fed. In cold weather fish eat nothing, so they should not be fed then. If the water is frozen over, the ice in one part of the pond must be broken every day. A pole or stout stick kept in the corner helps to keep a hole open, if it is waggled several times in daylight hours in frosty weather.

Some people are unlucky enough to lose their goldfish quickly because the creatures have been spotted by a passing heron or, in more rural areas, by another fish-eating bird, the kingfisher. This is likely to be partly due to the fact that the cover provided by the water plants is insufficient although, of course, there are bound to be times when all fish leave their shelter to bask in the sun. The pond can be covered over with wire netting which, if the mesh is fine enough, certainly keeps these birds off, but is also unsightly. It seems better to take a chance on the kingfishers, which are scarce now anyhow, and to keep the herons away by putting a single strand of plain wire about 30 cm (1 ft) high all round the perimeter of the pond. This can be linked to posts hidden behind the marginal plants, although they must be carefully placed so that they do not pierce the edging of the butyl rubber sheeting.

WILDLIFE IN THE POND

A few water snails can be introduced to add to the interest of the pond; they are good scavengers, keeping the pond clean, although they cannot be expected to clear up great amounts of pond scum. Water snails lay jelly-covered eggs on the underside of the leaves of aquatic plants and these are good food for fish and some of the other carnivorous water creatures, such as the aquatic larvae of dragonflies.

A variety of insects will visit the pond and children should look daily in spring and summer to see if any water boatmen have arrived: these scull along the surface on their backs. Pond-skaters are other interesting insects which move rapidly on the surface. Whirligig beetles, so-called because they dart about and always move in circles on top of the water, may also be seen: they have rounded, black backs and are only about 0·7 cm (3/10 in) long. The shallow edge of the pond is useful to thirsty flying insects, like bees and some butterflies, as well as providing for the entrance and exit of such interesting visitors as water spiders. Other visitors to look out for include adult dragonflies and caddis flies which can fly direct to weeds on the edge or growing out of the water.

Some amphibians may also visit the pond. These creatures breed in water, although they do not live in it all the year round. They climb out directly they are ready to leave and find sheltered, moist corners where they can live undisturbed.

Birds that come to drink from the shallow end of the pond may bring in small water creatures, or their eggs, on their legs and feet. These can be nearly invisible to the naked eye but sometimes it is just possible, in good lights, to see hordes of them moving in the water and they provide excellent food for fish. The commonest of them are called *Daphnia*, or non-biting water fleas, and *Cyclops*, which are one-eyed and helped in their movements by antennae or feelers. Both of these minute water creatures breed very rapidly. A few could be caught by children in a glass tube to be examined through a hand lens and subsequently put back into the water.

A MINIATURE WATER GARDEN

If there is no room for a full-size pool, it is possible to make a miniature water garden by sinking a wide, shallow plastic bath, or bowl into the ground. Tubs are too deep and can form death-traps to birds which go to drink and then slip or fall in. They are also difficult to keep clean and are liable to smell. It is actually possible to use polythene sheeting to line almost any small-sized pool, as long as the sheeting is cut with a wide enough margin to form a surround, as in the larger pools, which can be held down by flat stones. Really small, shallow pools, say 30 by 45 cm (1 by 1½ ft) could be used for the study of very small floating plants, like water fern (*Azolla caroliniana*), frogbit (*Hydrocharis morsus-ranae*) or even the duckweeds, as these all have interesting self-propagating methods of growth. Miniature pools must be watched carefully after very heavy showers which may flood them and during hot dry periods when they are liable to dry out. Pools of this size are not suitable for goldfish.

GARDENING NOTEBOOK

1. Make short notes about your pond-making experiences, putting in especially any unexpected difficulties or successes.
2. Add planting records to your diary page.
3. Look out for all visitors. Hedgehogs are creatures of habit and may

come to drink at the same time each day. Insects and other small creatures may be more difficult to identify but see p. 161 for the name of a useful freshwater plant and animal book. Add the names of visiting creatures to the list already started.

4. Look out too for water plants in other gardens. Some of the bigger lakes in parks and large gardens have water lilies and other foreign plants. Try to see whether plants are marginal, oxygenating or floating, and make lists of their names for your notebook, together with some sketches and photographs.

FURTHER TOPICS FOR DISCUSSION, OBSERVATION AND RESEARCH

1. Many of the water plants die right back in the winter. Some, like the floating frogbit (*Hydrocharis morsus-ranae*), produce winter buds which break off from the parent plant in the autumn and fall to the bottom of the pond. In the spring these buds rise to the surface and send dangling roots down before opening up and producing new young leaves. Try to find out how other water plants survive to provide fresh growth after appearing to be dead through the cold, dark winter.

2. Amphibians are now very scarce creatures. There is a great shortage of ponds in the countryside and anything that can be done to give these useful and interesting creatures a chance to survive is helpful. Discuss how places can be provided in which amphibians can breed, bearing in mind that they mate then lay their eggs and leave them to develop in the water, and need undisturbed damp places where they can spend the rest of the year.

3. Large ponds, lakes or wildfowl parks may have various water fowl swimming on them. Look particularly at their feet which may be webbed to help them dive and swim. Try to find out, by asking keepers or wardens, what the birds feed on. Collect pictures of some of these water birds.

9 · Trees and shrubs in the garden

Trees are an important part of the landscape. They beautify both countryside and town, adding interesting shapes (Fig. 26) and patterns and giving an extra dimension to flat ground. Some trees, like poplars, with long leaf stems and flat, undivided leaf blades, can add pleasing sounds in gardens as their leaves are moved by even the softest breeze.

They provide shelter and shade for both people and wildlife, giving cover to birds of many kinds as they can be used for roosting, as well as daylight perching places. They provide food if they produce berries or other edible fruit. Tree tops make useful look-out places above ground level from which birds can survey the surrounding area for their enemies, including birds of prey, like owls and hawks, and magpies, crows and jackdaws at nesting time; they can also keep a watch for grey squirrels and rats.

During the breeding season many birds use trees as nesting places and, as birds of the same kind are always ready to trespass and take over each other's territories, they also warn intending invaders to keep off. They do this by using trees and higher buildings as songposts, the cock bird loudly shouting out his particular tune to proclaim his tenancy. Bereaved or unmated cock birds sometimes sing loudly from the tops of trees for a mate.

Trees make essential windbreaks in exposed places, form shelter belts to hide ugly buildings and, if they are planted thickly enough, can also be helpful in improving the atmosphere as they add oxygen to the air during the daytime.

During the past quarter of a century, when there have been so many changes of land use in Britain, it is believed that over 20 million trees have been lost. Many have been felled during land-clearance operations or have died after land has been drained. Others have died from disease; the present epidemic of Dutch elm disease has spread rapidly through most of the country because the fungus that kills the elms is carried by flying elm bark beetles and also because diseased timber has been transported from one area to another.

Because of this great loss, it is now more important than ever that more trees should be planted wherever there is suitable space for them. Gardens, school yards or the edges of playing fields are good places as they

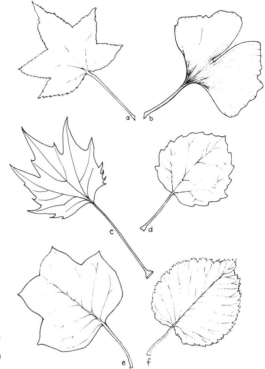

24. *Six tree-leaf shapes*

a Sweet gum *(Liquidamber styraciflua)*
b Maidenhair tree *(Ginkgo biloba)*
c London plane *(Platanus × hispanica)*
d Aspen *(Populus tremula)*
e Tulip-tree *(Liriodendron tulipifera)*
f English elm *(Ulmus procera)*

are not usually subject to disturbance and the trees can grow without interference. Many national tree-growing organisations, including the Forestry Commission (see p. 166), as well as local groups are now being formed to improve the neighbourhood landscape and would welcome help and interest from children, as well as from adults.

PROPAGATING TREES AND SHRUBS

All wild trees and shrubs produce seed in the autumn and children can collect some for planting. There are different kinds of oaks, and acorns can be picked up from the ground underneath them (see also p. 144). They can pick up a few seeds from beneath other trees too, such as keys from ash trees, triangular nuts in prickly cases from beeches, rounded, shiny conkers from horse chestnuts and double winged sycamore fruits. In a coniferous wood, closed-up pine or spruce cones can often be found;

a London plane *(Platanus x hispanica)*
b Sycamore *(Acer pseudoplatanus)*
c Horse chestnut *(Aesculus hippocastanum)*
d Acorn, English oak *(Quercus robur)*
e Acorn, Turkey oak *(Quercus cerris)*
f Acorn, Holm oak *(Quercus ilex)*

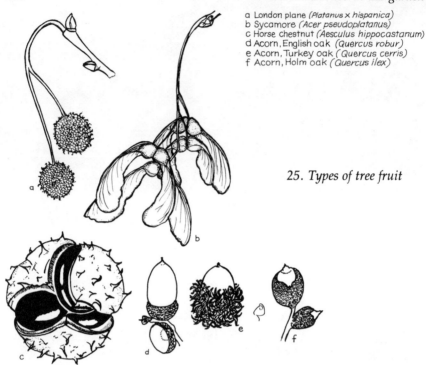

25. *Types of tree fruit*

these open up when they are dry and then their papery-winged seeds fall out. Berries from hawthorns and rowans (mountain ash) are simple to grow, provided they are ripe when planted.

The various seeds should be put into pots of dampened seed compost (see p. 42). A different pot should be used for each species of tree seed and each container should be labelled with the name of the tree under which the seed was found and the date. The best guide to planting these seeds is to sow them to a depth of only about three times their own thickness. Some of the tree seeds will germinate faster than others (see p. 51), while some may not start growing until the following spring and others may take still longer, so patience will be required. The soil in the pots should be kept damp as the seeds will never germinate if they dry out. When the tree seedlings have two true leaves, as well as their seed leaves or cotyledons, they can be planted out, either in a bigger pot, using one seedling to a 15 cm (6 in) pot, or straight into the ground. It must be remembered, however, that a small seedling may, in a few years' time, develop into a tree that has grown far too large for its original site, and that moving trees can be a tricky and expensive business. Young trees grown from seed should not be thrown away, suitable areas should be found for them where they can develop undisturbed. It is worth asking advice from the Forestry Commission.

Growing trees from seed, especially coniferous trees like pines, spruces, Douglas firs and thuyas, is part of the Forestry Commission's work. Foresters look after huge seed beds in special tree nurseries and it is sometimes possible to arrange for parties to visit. The Forestry Commission is anxious to help to increase children's interest in trees and has many schemes for visitors of all ages. They will also supply schools with tree seedlings for planting and growing-on. Useful booklets and other information are available from their headquarters (see p. 166).

Instead of using seed, growers and nurserymen frequently grow trees and shrubs from cuttings as described in Chapter 4. The easiest of all trees to grow from cuttings are willows and poplars. Twigs from most species of these two will send out stem roots if they are just put into water after being cut from the tree. The rooted cuttings can then be planted out into a pot containing growing compost. Other cuttings vary in their ease of rooting. Some get away very easily, others need a lot of patience and can be helped by having their cut ends dipped into hormone rooting powder.

Grafting, also referred to in Chapter 4, is another method of propagating trees used by professional or expert gardeners. It is usually necessary to graft plants that do not come true from seeds or do not take well from cuttings. Many fruit and other ornamental trees are grafted to combine the desirable characteristics of the rootstock and scion and to minimise their disadvantages. Many trees and shrubs can also be propagated by layering.

CHOOSING TREES FOR THE GARDEN

Whether children are growing their own trees from seeds, cuttings or layers, or wish to buy one which is already several feet tall, there are many factors to consider before deciding which type to have. It is important, for example, to take into consideration the rate of growth and final size of the tree in relation to the space available for it. It is no good planting a giant, such as an oak, in a tiny garden, because it will take all the light as it grows and its roots will absorb a great deal of nourishment from a wide area of the surrounding soil. Tree roots take up as much room underground as their leafy branches or crowns do overhead: the height of a tree can increase rapidly and its root system will develop equally quickly.

Most of the wild trees which can be grown from seed will become too large for the average garden but they are still fun to grow and very rewarding as long as the warning given about their eventual size is heeded.

Before choosing trees, other gardens in the same neighbourhood should be observed to see which trees are growing successfully. It may also be possible to ask the garden owners their reasons for growing these trees.

Some trees thrive particularly well in built-up locations where the atmosphere may still be slightly polluted. The following would be suitable for industrial areas and cities:

beeches (*Fagus* spp); birches (*Betula* spp); cherries (*Prunus* spp); crab apples (*Malus* spp); *Eucalyptus* spp; honey locust (*Gleditsia tricanthos*); Indian bean tree (*Catalpa bignonioides*); London plane (*Platanus* × *hispanica*); pears (*Pyrus* spp); poplars (*Populus* spp); tree of heaven (*Ailanthus altissima*); willows (*Salix* spp).

As well as being leafy shade givers, some trees produce attractive blossom and there is a wide choice of ornamental flowering trees. It is not a good idea to be tempted into buying trees with double flowers, however beautiful they may look during their brief flowering period. They are non-productive, in that they produce no fruit and are not attractive to bees or other pollinating insects (see p. 31).

Apart from the final size of the tree, its shape and appearance should be

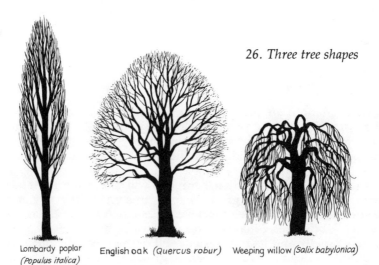

26. Three tree shapes

Lombardy poplar
(Populus italica)

English oak *(Quercus robur)*

Weeping willow *(Salix babylonica)*

taken into account. Particularly suitable for smaller gardens are the so-called fastigiate trees. These have tall, thin, erect branches and take up far less space than the more usual, spreading types. Where space is not a problem weeping trees with pendulous branches which make a leafy bower are very popular. Two favourites are the weeping willow (*Salix babylonica*) and the silver-leaved pear (*Pyrus salicifolia* 'Pendula').

Where only one tree can be planted it is a good idea to choose a multi-purpose type. Many fruit trees come under this heading as they give beauty in their leaves and blossom as well as producing fruit and shading part of the garden. Apple, pear, cherry and plum trees can all be grown as standard, many-branched trees or as specially trained specimens to grow against walls or in narrow rows. These trained types do, however, need careful attention and pruning to keep their shape.

Berry-producing trees, like the rowans or mountain ashes (*Sorbus aucuparia* cultivars), hawthorns (*Crataegus* spp) and cotoneasters (*Cotoneaster* spp), are also good in gardens as they produce ornamental fruit, much enjoyed by birds in early winter, after a profusion of flowers in the spring or summer. The various crab apples (*Malus sylvestris* cultivars) too, have fruit that is delightful to look at and which can be made into good, edible jelly, as well as pleasing the birds.

There is also a wide range of foliage shapes and colours to choose from. Many trees have pleasant green leaves in the spring and summer, which turn to brilliant hues of red, yellow, orange or brown in the autumn. These are a particular asset in the garden at a time of the year when there is less colour from flowers. Some genera which contain trees with good autumn colour are:

Acer (sycamore and maple); *Betula* (birch); *Crataegus* (hawthorn); *Fagus* (beech); *Liquidamber* (sweet gum); *Malus* (apple); *Populus* (poplar); *Prunus* (cherry); *Quercus* (oak); *Sorbus* (rowan and whitebeam).

Many trees have foliage in colours other than green. Some have variegated leaves which are marked with patches of white, cream or yellow. Where there are several green-leaved trees in the garden or immediate neighbourhood these can make a refreshing change but more than one should not be planted or their value as an outstanding trees will be lost. Some trees with unusual coloured foliage are:

RED OR PURPLE LEAVES *Acer palmatum* 'Atropurpureum'; *Acer platanoides* 'Crimson King'; *Fagus sylvatica purpurea*; *Fagus sylvatica* 'Riversii'; *Liquidamber styraciflua*; *Malus* 'Profusion'; *Malus × purpurea*; *Prunus cerasifera* 'Trailblazer'; *Prunus × cistena*.
YELLOW LEAVES *Acer negundo* 'Auratum'; *Acer pseudoplatanus*

'Worleei'; *Gleditsia tricanthos* 'Sunburst'; *Populus* 'Serotina Alba'; *Robinia pseudoacacia* 'Frisia'.

GREY OR SILVER LEAVES   *Eucalyptus* spp; *Populus alba*; *Pyrus* spp; *Salix alba*; *Sorbus aria* 'Lutescens'.

VARIEGATED LEAVES   *Acer variegatum*; *Acer platanoides* 'Drummondii'; *Acer pseudoplatanus* 'Leopoldii'; *Platanus* × *hispanica* 'Suttneri'; *Populus* × *candicans* 'Aurora'.

Some variation in effect can also be obtained by using trees with unusual or ornamental bark. Some genera which include such trees are:

Acer (particularly *AA. griseum* and *grosseri*); *Betula*; *Eucalyptus*; *Platanus*; *Prunus*; *Salix*.

Many of the trees which have been mentioned so far are deciduous. Evergreen trees are never completely leafless although they discard a few old leaves all the year round and start to grow new ones in the spring. The majority of evergreen trees are coniferous (or cone-bearing) species such as pines, spruces, firs and junipers. It is worthwhile including one or two evergreens in the garden, if there is room, as they add winter colour. Some conifers will form dwarf specimen trees which can be especially suitable for rock gardens and some can also be grown in containers (see Chapter 7).

SITING THE TREE

Before buying a tree it is essential to give serious consideration to the choice of a site for it in the garden. Obviously places where there are drainage pipes or underground or overhead cables should be avoided. Nor should the tree be planted too near buildings or fences as there will be insufficient light and soil for it to grow properly and it may also upset neighbours as it gets bigger. It should not be planted too near to other trees either and, as explained on p. 113, its final size *must* be borne in mind when selecting a site. The new tree may seem to have plenty of room now but in ten years' time could have outgrown the space available to it.

PLANTING

The best times of the year in which to plant trees are the autumn and winter, although those which are bought growing in a container can be planted throughout the year if necessary. Establishing container-grown trees in the summer can be tricky, especially if the weather is hot and dry, as they will need to be given large, regular amounts of water for a month or more after planting. In the winter the trees are dormant so transplanting them will not have such a serious effect on their growth.

Once the tree has been bought, a hole wider and deeper than its root spread should be dug. The soil at the bottom should be broken up and some peat mixed in with it. This will enable the roots to penetrate more easily at first. Any young tree over 1·2 m (4 ft) tall needs to be tied to a stake to give it some support. The stake should be at least one-third of the tree's height and should be inserted firmly in the hole before the tree is planted so that the roots are not damaged by it.

Two people are needed to plant a tree—one to hold it steady and upright and the other to fill the hole with soil. The tree should be held in the centre of the hole with the soil mark (the level the soil reached before the tree was moved) on the trunk level with the ground. The tree should be shaken gently once or twice so that the roots fall into their normal growing pattern. Then the hole should be gradually filled in, shaking the roots again very gently at first to make sure that all the spaces are filled. Once the soil is level with the surrounding ground it should be trodden down firmly all round, especially close to the trunk, and the soil level made up again if necessary.

The stake should be tied to the trunk by a narrow, plastic tree tie: these are obtainable from garden centres and should be used according to the instructions. The tie should not be too tight round the trunk and the stake should always remain parallel to it and vertical.

AFTERCARE

The soil round the tree should be mounded up towards the trunk and then mulched with fallen leaves, grass mowings or compost immediately after planting. This top cover should be renewed as necessary as birds frequently disturb it by scratching about for insects and other food.

The new tree should be watered regularly, at least at weekly intervals in dry periods, for although the mulch will help to conserve moisture in the soil near the top, it is very important that all the roots also have moist soil in which to grow. They must never dry out. Fertilisers should not be used until the tree has been in for at least a year. They should not really be necessary even then, provided the tree was planted properly, the top mulch is watched and the watering is carried out carefully. The stake should be checked frequently, especially after rough weather, making sure that the tie is never constricting the trunk, pulling it out of alignment or rubbing it in any way.

Pruning, in the form of cutting back the tips of the new young tree's branches to encourage the production of more branches, should not be done until March, if the tree was planted in the previous autumn, and, if spring planted, can be left until the following spring. Some gardeners do no pruning at all in the first year. Subsequent pruning depends entirely on the amount of growth that the tree has made and the shape of tree that is ultimately being sought. All trees need different pruning: the subject is quite complex and needs thoughtful study and is therefore not a task for younger children.

SHRUBS

These are plants growing from woody stems which produce bushes ranging in height from only a few centimentres up to 3 m (10 ft) or more. Unlike trees, they do not have one straight trunk and are distinguished from herbaceous plants by having woody growth which does not die back each winter. There is a tremendous range of garden shrubs to choose from. They can be planted to fulfil many purposes but are chosen mainly for their beauty and often for the fragrance of their flowers and their interest to butterflies and bees. Below is a short list of a few favourite flowering shrubs.

SHRUB	FLOWERING SEASON	COMMENTS
Beauty bush (*Kolkwitzia amabilis*)	May to August	Plentiful pink flowers. A shrub of particular beauty, as its name suggests.
Brooms (*Cytisus* and *Genista* spp)	April to September	Pea-shaped flowers, variety of colours but often yellow.
Camellia spp and cultivars	February to April	Pink, red, white or bi-coloured flowers. Not for alkaline soils.
Ceanothus spp	May to October	Exceptionally striking blue flowers. Not fully hardy.
Flowering currants (*Ribes sanguineum* and *odoratum*)	April	*Sanguineum* red flowers, *odoratum* yellow.
Forsythia 'Robusta' and other cultivars	March to April	Yellow flowers. A reliable shrub for early spring.
Hardy plumbago (*Ceratostigma wilmottianum*)	June to September	Brilliant blue flowers and red leaves.
Heaths and heathers (*Erica* and *Calluna* spp)	All year round if cultivars chosen carefully	Flowers white and shades of pink and purple. Many cultivars have very attractive coloured foliage, some in shades of bronze and gold. Only EE. *herbacea* (*carnea*) and × *darleyensis* for alkaline soils.

SHRUB	FLOWERING SEASON	COMMENTS
Hebe, various spp and hybrids	May to September	Flowers white, pink, and shades of blue and mauve. Not always hardy but good for coastal areas.
Hydrangea spp	July to September	Flowers white, pink and shades of blue and mauve. Especially recommended for coastal areas.
Lilacs (*Syringa vulgaris* cultivars)	May to June	White, mauve and purple flowers. Sweetly scented.
Magnolia spp	April to June	Flowers usually white, sometimes creamy or flushed with pink. Most dislike alkaline soils.
Mock orange (*Philadelphus* spp)	April to July	Plentiful white flowers, strongly scented.
Rhododendron (including *Azalea*) spp and cultivars	March to June	A wide variety of colours, some soft, some brilliant; most azaleas strongly scented. Often with contrasting spots or patches on flowers, which act as honey guides. Not for alkaline soils.
Roses (*Rosa* spp and cultivars)	May to October	Grown for their profusion of flowers in a wide range of colours and often for their sweet scent. Fruits (hips) frequently very attractive.
Summer jasmine (*Jasminum officinale*)	July to October	White flowers, sweetly scented.
Sun roses (*Cistus* spp)	June to September	White, pink or red flowers, some with contrasting central blotch which acts as a honey guide. Needs sunny position.
Weigela (various cultivars, including the popular *W. florida* 'Variegata', and hybrids)	May to July	A particularly attractive hardy shrub with creamy, pink or red flowers. *W.f.* 'Variegata' has leaves of soft green, edged with creamy white.

Many shrubs have leaves of unusual colour, for example the purple smoke bush (*Cotinus coggygria*) and the purple-leaved barberry (*Berberis thunbergii atropurpurea*). Evergreen shrubs, like yellow-flowered mahonias (*MM. aquifolium* and *japonica*) and Mexican orange (*Choisya ternata*) with shiny bright green leaves and the variegated evergreen privet—to give it a popular misnomer—(*Euonymus japonicus*), are also helpful in giving the garden winter interest.

The evergreen 'privet' and a deciduous privet (*Ligustrum ovalifolium)* as well as a fuchsia (*F. magellanica*), various briar roses, firethorns (*Pyracantha* spp), *Cotoneaster* spp and various hollies (*Ilex* spp) can also be used for hedging and screening purposes. Many of them provide flowers with nectar for insects, shelter for birds and scaffolding for web-spinning spiders which are helpful in the garden to keep flies down.

Some shrubs also produce attractive berries in the autumn. Others, like the scarlet willow (*Salix alba* 'Chermesina'), the golden willow (*Salix alba* 'Vitellina'), the red-twigged Westonbirt dogwood (*Cornus alba* 'Sibirica') and the green-twigged Himalayan honeysuckle (*Leycesteria formosa*) can add colour to a garden because of their variously shaded twigs; these show up particularly well after the leaves have fallen. Some shrubs provide autumn colouring as well as flowers at other times of the year. The witch hazels (*Hamamelis* spp) and the modern hybrid azaleas can have beautifully colourful autumn leaves.

There are other shrubs which add great winter attraction to gardens by providing colour in the darkest months, from December until February. Here are some, with reasons for growing them:

bush willow (*Salix fargesii*) (big red buds); Christmas box (*Sarcococca humilis*) (fragrant white flowers); evergreen clematis (*Clematis cirrhosa balearica*) (interesting green flowers); garland flower (*Daphne odora* 'Aureomarginata') (purple-centred fragrant white flowers); heathers (*Erica herbacea* (*carnea*) and × *darleyensis* cultivars) (wide range of colours in foliage and flowers); honeysuckles (*Lonicera fragrantissima*, × *purpusii* and *L. standishii*) (fragrant creamy-white flowers); red willow (*Salix daphnoides*) (dark reddish-purple stems); silk tassel bush (*Garrya elliptica*) (green catkins); winter jasmine (*Jasminum nudiflorum*) (yellow flowers); wintersweet (*Chimonanthus praecox*) (fragrant white flowers); witch hazels (*Hammamelis mollis* and other spp) (very early yellow fragrant flowers).

The size of shrubs ranges from those that are prostrate, or very low, like the fishbone cotoneaster (*C. horizontalis*) and rose of Sharon (*Hypericum calycinum*), which can be used as ground-cover plants (see p. 84), up to those that grow very tall and almost tree-like. As with trees, young gardeners should make sure of the final heights and widths of various shrubs before making up their minds which to choose. In fact, it would be well worth their while spending some time looking around in gardens, parks and nurseries at different times of the year to see the types that are available and decide which would be suitable for the garden. Before making the final choice it is also important to make sure that any new ones will complement existing trees and shrubs and the layout of the garden.

On the whole most shrubs only need maintenance pruning. This means that excessive growth should be removed neatly and any dead wood cut out. As mentioned earlier, pruning is a very complex subject. Its timing will depend on the flowering habits of the shrub in question—whether it produces its flowers on new young shoots or on older branches—and it is as well to take expert advice.

GARDENING NOTEBOOK

1. If you plant a grown tree or shrub, write a description of your reasons for the choice and then describe all you did to settle it in well. Also add any planting records to the diary page.

2. Collect leaves and look carefully at their shapes; notice that some have only one leaf blade and others have several leaflets. Note also whether their edges, or margins, are smooth or scalloped, toothed or notched. Draw some leaves for your notebook and make patterns and designs from others (see Fig. 24).

3. While looking at trees, especially in the winter when the deciduous ones are bare, look out for mistletoe growing from limes, poplars, hawthorns and other trees. Mistletoe (*Viscum album*) is a tree parasite and is sown by birds, often mistle thrushes, which clean their bills and so wipe the sticky berries on to the tree's bark, where they sometimes start growing. Make notes of the names of the trees and places where you see mistletoe growing and make a sketch of a small piece of mistletoe. It has separately sexed flowers growing on different plants (see p. 88).

4. Try to identify trees from their shapes in winter.

5. Notice trees' barks. Some are smooth, some exceedingly rough and some, like planes, are flaky. Bark rubbings can be made, with cobbler's wax, to show different bark patterns and can then be used as moulds for making plaster of Paris models. These can be appropriately coloured with poster-paints to make artificial bark. Make a list of trees with outstanding interestingly patterned or coloured bark.

6. Draw and paint some variegated leaves to show their patterns.

FURTHER TOPICS FOR DISCUSSION, OBSERVATION AND RESEARCH

1. Trees can vary in size when they are fully grown from the dwarf Noah's ark juniper (*Juniperus communis* 'Compressa'), which may never reach more than 30 cm (1 ft) high, to the huge giant coast redwood (*Sequoia sempervirens*). The tallest of these, over 61 m (200 ft), is called Howard Libbey and it grows in California among other slightly lesser giants. Find out more about these giant trees and also some of the heights of the tallest trees in this country (see p. 163).

2. Discuss the uses of timber and read some of the Forestry Commission's leaflets. They will send them to anyone who is interested (see p. 166).

3. Most conifers are evergreens but there are a few which lose their leaves in the winter. Larches (*Larix* spp), dawn redwood (*Metasequoia stroboides*) and swamp cypresses (*Taxodium* spp) are deciduous conifers. Try to find some and draw and colour in their twigs in different seasons.

10 · Visiting parks and gardens

There are usually plenty of places where it is possible for children to study plants, whether they live in the town or the country. When deciding on which plants to grow, visits could be made to local nurseries and garden centres and, to see how they can be used to best effect, some of the many parks and gardens open to the public could also be viewed.

BOTANIC GARDENS

The most famous collections of both British and foreign plants in this country are in botanic gardens. The best known of these include the Royal Botanic Gardens at Kew, near Richmond in Surrey, its satellite country garden at Wakehurst Place, near Haywards Heath in Sussex, and also in Edinburgh, and those at Oxford and Cambridge. There are botanic gardens in many other university towns and in our bigger cities and most of them are open every day.

PUBLIC PARKS

There are also plenty of public parks that are open throughout the year. Some of them contain interesting, and even uncommon, trees and other plants.

The idea of special parks kept for public use is not very old and, in fact, some of the oldest, founded last century, were often named after Queen Victoria. If they were constructed later many were named after the monarch reigning at the time. Some of these, particularly those named after royalty, are formal parks with laid-out paths and flower beds to give visitors the pleasure of walking round and seeing colourful displays of well-grown and carefully tended flowering plants at all seasons.

Other public parks, which may be less formal but have other interesting features, may once have been large private gardens. These sometimes surround large houses that are now being used as institutions of various kinds and offices. In this type of park there are often lofty glass orangeries or palm houses. They were built to grow such interesting exotic plants as orange, lemon and banana trees, palms, orchids, cacti and succulents which were being brought to this country from abroad by returning travellers. Particularly fine examples of orangeries can be seen at the Royal Botanic Gardens, Kew, and Syon House, Brentford, Middlesex.

It is often interesting for young, as well as older, gardeners to find out the history of the parks they visit, particularly in their local area, to see why they were first constructed, how they were laid out and by whom.

GARDENS

Many beautiful gardens are opened to the public each year, most of them in aid of charity, so a small entrance fee is often charged. Some are at their best in the spring, others in the summer and there are also gardens where autumn tree colour is particularly fine.

Particulars of these gardens can usually be found in public libraries. They will probably have the National Gardens Scheme's booklet *Gardens of England and Wales* which contains information about the times the gardens are open, as well as other material about the garden schemes for Scotland, Ulster and Eire. Certain gardens owned by the National Trust are opened to the public to support the National Gardens Scheme and these and many more can be found in *The Historic Houses, Castles and Gardens in Great Britain and Ireland* from ABC Historic Publications. Other gardens are open to the public for a small entrance fee in aid of the Gardeners' Sunday Organisation and are described in their booklet called *Gardens to Visit*.

A selection of these gardens which have particularly interesting features is given on p. 127 although there has only been room to include a few of the hundreds of beautiful places that are open to the public.

Children will find that it is a good idea to take a notebook when visiting gardens and make rough notes, rather than trying to rely on memory when they return.

Garden design

The history of garden design is a long and fascinating one as garden designers or landscapers have been advising owners about the layout of their land for centuries. Some had travelled abroad and brought back ideas from other countries. These more formal influences were more noticeable before the eighteenth century.

In France, gardens were often laid out in extremely complicated, geometric designs. Such formal flower-bed arrangements, frequently on one level, were known as parterres and here low-growing plants were used to produce coloured, patterned 'carpets'. Carpet bedding is still popular in our parks although less so today as its labour cost is so high. Designs based on these earlier patterns and some more modern ones, such as coats of arms and floral clocks, can sometimes be seen in resorts such as Blackpool and Brighton.

Italian gardens were famous for their terraces, with wide, ornamental stone staircases leading up and down from one level to another, and delightful, pointed cypress trees.

Some garden landscapers seem to have enjoyed planning all kinds of little buildings like temples and summer houses, a number of which were adorned by statues of classical gods and goddesses. Vast fountains and fountain courts, as well as tall towers or turrets, were also constructed as garden ornaments. When these towers were placed on slopes among trees to be used as look-out places, they were known as gazebos.

The owners of these gardens appear to have vied with each other to build more and more decorative grottoes with tunnels and shell houses, or caves through which water dripped and where non-flowering plants like ferns grew lushly in the damp surroundings. Follies, so called because they were thought to be foolish, useless buildings and a waste of money, were also designed as garden improvements although some owners had them built in order to give the labourers employment.

In the eighteenth century, more natural-looking landscapes were preferred, although many of these earlier fancy features were kept. William Kent, and after him Lancelot, or 'Capability', Brown, both very famous garden designers, planted trees in groups, clumps or sometimes as solitary specimens to add beauty to wide, grassy rides or open stretches of land. Some rich landowners had valleys dammed to make huge lakes or long, river-like reaches of water, and several were surrounded by banks of trees and flowering shrubs. Stourhead, in Wiltshire, is a particularly fine example of this kind of garden.

Because many of these large gardens were surrounded by meadows and fields where horses, sheep, cattle or deer grazed, it was necessary to find some way to keep the animals from straying into the decoratively planted areas. Ugly fences or high walls were out of place in the new,

27. *Some examples of topiary*

natural garden layouts; they were artificial features which would spoil the view. So a sunken cutting or ha-ha was invented. This was a wide, deep, empty dyke or ditch with a high vertical side nearer the garden which hardly showed from a distance. Ha-has were often used and can still be seen today. They are said to have got their curious name because strangers, strolling in the garden, came across them suddenly and were so astonished to find the hidden boundary that they exclaimed 'Ha-ha!'

Old gardens will sometimes contain fine examples of topiary. Topiaried trees and shrubs are those which have had their crowns or the whole of their leaf-bearing branches chopped or pruned into all kinds of shapes.

Other aspects of interest

HISTORY   When visiting gardens that surround castles, palaces, mansions and smaller old houses encourage childen to decide if the gardens match, or try to match, the architectural styles of the buildings. This will involve their finding out more about the history of buildings as well as garden design.

At the Roman Palace, at Fishbourne, near Chichester in Sussex, the garden has been excavated and planted up with plants known to have been grown by the Romans who lived there. Parts of the garden at Hampton Court, near London, have some redesigned formal-hedged flower beds and an Elizabethan knot garden, even though this part of the large garden was only laid out earlier this century. Also at Hampton Court is the famous maze. This is a high, clipped hornbeam hedge surrounding a puzzle walk; other mazes may have yew or beech hedges bordering the paths.

PLANTS   Some gardens in towns may be very small, so may those belonging to cottages in country villages, but they are often full of colourful plants. Point out how every bit of space in these gardens is used to the best advantage and encourage the young gardeners to find out the names of any flowers they do not recognise.

The different ways of using colour in the garden could also be studied. For example, there are special white and silver, red, and soft mauve and blue borders at Sissinghurst Castle, in Kent, and a particularly fine mixed-colour herbaceous border at Polesden Lacey, near Dorking in Surrey. Long and wide herbaceous borders involve a lot of work and the more modern idea of having island beds makes it easier to look after individual plants when they are close-planted to give bright splashes of colour. Examples of these can be seen at the Royal Horticultural Society's gardens at Wisley, in Surrey, and in an increasing number of private and public parks.

Some public parks and private gardens contain special collections of

trees. These are known as arboreta (singular—arboretum) and a list of
some interesting ones to visit is given on p. 129.

PRACTICAL HINTS   No parts of the gardens that are being visited
should be passed by casually. Instead the different ways in which plants
are grown should be noticed and commented on. For instance, many
plants have to be supported by various types of stake to prevent them
from falling or being blown over. Labour-saving ideas should also be
looked for. More and more flowering shrubs, which do not need as much
attention as bedding-out plants and flower borders, are now being
grown. But it may be necessary to weed round the shrubs, especially if
they grow well above the ground, so the use of different types of ground-
cover plants could be studied too (see p. 84).

Walled gardens should be carefully observed by children, and in particular the way in which the walls have been used for growing different
trees and climbers, so that they get maximum light, support and protection, as well as using all the available vertical space. Rock gardens may
need to be searched for as they are not always in the same part of the
garden as the more formal lawns, flower beds and other features. The use
of tufa rock is particularly interesting here, especially as a lightweight
material, as is the use of peat blocks; (see pp. 86 and 99). There is a
gardener living in the middle of Birmingham who has a big tufa rock cliff
on which he grows alpines.

SOIL AND LANDSCAPE   It is important to look at the soil and to assess
its type wherever possible. Many of the most famous gardens are on light,
sandy, acid soils which suit rhododendrons, camellias, heathers, heaths
and other beautiful shrubs and trees that turn brilliant colours in the
autumn. The Savill Gardens in Windsor Great Park are an example of this
kind of garden. Here the blue-flowered Himalayan poppies flourish and
make a brilliant contrast in early summer with all the reds, pinks, oranges,
golds and yellows of the rhododendrons and azaleas. Natural features
within the garden, such as slopes and hollows, should also be discussed.

Children should also be encouraged to study the surroundings of the
different gardens. Does a town garden make the visitor forget how close
he is to other houses, roads and the noise from traffic? Does the country
garden greatly improve the natural landscape by adding fresh features?

Although young visitors should be critical about the gardens they see,
they should, above all, learn something interesting and fresh which they
can put into practice at home.

SOME GARDENS WHICH EXHIBIT PARTICULARLY INTERESTING FEATURES

Gardens originally laid out by famous designers

'CAPABILITY' BROWN   Blenheim Palace, Woodstock, Oxfordshire; Broadlands, Romsey, Hampshire; Luton Hoo, Bedfordshire; The Rhododendron Dell, Kew, Surrey.

GERTRUDE JEKYLL   Littlehay, Burley, New Forest, Hampshire.

WILLIAM KENT   Holkham, Norfolk.

AMATEUR OWNER, FOLLOWING KENT'S STYLE   Stourhead, Stourton, Wiltshire.

SIR JOSEPH PAXTON   Elcot Park, Newbury, Berkshire.

HUMPHREY REPTON   Bolwick Hall, Norwich, Norfolk; Sezincote, Moreton-in-Marsh, Gloucestershire; Sheringham Hall, Norfolk; West Wycombe Park, Buckinghamshire.

WILLIAM ROBINSON   Gravetye Manor, East Grinstead, West Sussex; Leckhampton, Cambridgeshire.

Gardens with special ornamental features

FOLLIES   Belmont Park, Throwley, Faversham, Kent; Benington Lordship, Hertfordshire.

FOUNTAINS   Brantwych Hall, Melbourn, Cambridgeshire; Chatsworth, Bakewell, Derbyshire; Pusey House, Faringdon, Oxfordshire.

GAZEBOS   Melford Hall, Sudbury, Suffolk; Montacute, Yeovil, Somerset; Stoneleigh Abbey, Kenilworth, Warwickshire.

GROTTOES   Belmont Park, Throwley, Faversham, Kent; Wellingham House, Ringmer, East Sussex.

HA-HAS   Notton Lodge, Lacock, Wiltshire; Parham Park, Pulborough, West Sussex; The Educational Museum, Haslemere, Surrey.

MULTIPLE GARDEN WITH MANY DIFFERENT LAYOUTS   Compton Acres, Poole, Dorset.

NATURAL ROCKY OUTCROPS   Penns-in-the-rocks, Groombridge, East Sussex.

ORANGERIES   Faringdon House, Berkshire; Ripple Hall, Tewkesbury, Gloucestershire; Royal Botanic Gardens, Kew, Surrey; Saltram House, Plympton, Devon; Somerset College of Agriculture and Horticulture, Cannington, Bridgwater, Somerset.

TEMPLES   St Paul's Walden Bury, Hitchin, Hertfordshire; Stourhead, Stourton, Wiltshire; Stowe School, Buckingham.

WATERFOWL   Barkham Manor, Wokingham, Berkshire; Bohunt, Liphook, Hampshire; The Limes, Apperknowle, Chesterfield, Derbyshire.

WATER-MILL   Duxford Mill, Cambridge.
WATER-WHEEL   Enys, Penryn, Cornwall.

Gardens with special plant features

ALPINES   Barnett Brook, Whitchurch, South Merseyside; Severn View, Grovesend, Gloucestershire.
CAMELLIA WALK   Melpash Court, Bridport, Dorset.
DWARF AND SLOW-GROWING CONIFERS   The Pygmy Pinetum, Hillworth Road, Devizes, Wiltshire.
FLOWER-ARRANGERS' PLANTS   Ashford Manor, Ludlow, Shropshire.
GROUND-COVER PLANTS   Tambramhill Gardens, Nottingham; The Margery Fish Nursery, East Lambrook Manor, South Petherton, Somerset.
HERB GARDENS   Longstock Park, Stockbridge, Hampshire; Pant-yr-Holiad, Rhydlewis, Llandysul, Dyfyd; Sissinghurst Castle, Kent; Troy, Ewelme, Oxfordshire.
HERBACEOUS BORDERS   Howbury Hall, Renhold, Bedford; Nymans, Handcross, West Sussex; Polesden Lacey, nr Dorking, Surrey; RHS Gardens, Wisley, Ripley, Surrey; Savill Gardens, Windsor Park, Berkshire.
KNOT GARDENS   Hampton Court Palace, East Molesey, Surrey; Hever Castle, Edenbridge, Kent; Ludstone Hall, Claverley, Wolverhampton, Shropshire; New Place, Stratford-on-Avon, Warwickshire.
MAGNOLIAS   Borde Hill, Haywards Heath, West Sussex; Coverwood, Ewhurst, Surrey; Nymans, Handcross, West Sussex.
MAZES   Glendurgan, Falmouth, Cornwall; Hampton Court Palace, East Molesey, Surrey; Harewood Hall, nr Harrogate, Yorkshire; Somerleyton Hall, Lowestoft, Suffolk.
PARTERRES   Blenheim Palace, Woodstock, Oxfordshire; Blickling Hall, Norwich, Norfolk; Chevening, Sevenoaks, Kent.
RHODODENDRONS AND AZALEAS   Bodnant, Tal y Cafn, Gwynedd, North Wales (look out also for the magnificent laburnum walk there); Glandyfi Castle, Machynlleth, Dyfyd; Knighthayes Court, Tiverton, Devon; Lanhydrock, Bodmin, Cornwall; Lea Rhododendron Garden, Matlock, Derbyshire; Leonardslee, Lower Beeding, West Sussex; Minterne, Cerne Abbas, Dorset.
TOPIARY   Great Dixter, Northiam, East Sussex; Hampton Court Palace, East Molesey, Surrey; St Nicholas, Richmond, Yorkshire.
WALLED GARDENS   Carrog, Aberystwyth, Dyfyd; Kissing Tree House, Alveston, Stratford-on-Avon, Warwickshire; Wenlock Abbey, Much Wenlock, Shropshire.

WATER GARDENS Cliveden, Cookham, Buckinghamshire; Brantwych Hall, Melbourn, Cambridgeshire.

ARBORETA

ENGLAND

Avon	Bath Botanic Gardens
Bedfordshire	Woburn Abbey
Berkshire	Windsor Great Park
Cornwall	Glendurgan, Falmouth
Devon	Bicton, East Budleigh
Dorset	Abbotsbury
Gloucestershire	Hidcote Manor, Chipping Campden; Westonbirt, Tetbury
Hampshire	Exbury, Beaulieu; Bordrewood, New Forest; Jermyns House, Ampfield; Rhinefield Terrace, New Forest
Herefordshire	Eastnor Castle, Ledbury
Isles of Scilly	Tresco Abbey
Kent	The National Pinetum, Bedgebury
Middlesex	Syon Park, Brentford
Surrey	Winkworth, Godalming
West Sussex	Borde Hill, Haywards Heath; Wakehurst Place, Ardingly; West Dean, Chichester
Wiltshire	Stourhead, Stourton

WALES

Gwynnedd	Bodnant Gardens, Tal-y-Cafn
Powys	Powis Castle, Welshpool

SCOTLAND

Argyll	Inveraray Castle; Royal Botanic Gardens, Edinburgh; Younger Botanic Garden, Benmore
Ayrshire	Culzean Castle, Girvan
Perthshire	Blair Castle, Blair Atholl; Doune House, Dunblane; Scone Palace, Perth
Wigtonshire	Castle Kennedy, Lochinch

NORTHERN IRELAND

Co Down	Castlewellan, Newcastle; Rowallane, Saintfield

REPUBLIC OF IRELAND

Dublin	Glasnevin Botanic Garden
Co Offaly	Birr Castle
Co Wexford	John F. Kennedy Memorial Arboretum, New Ross (young trees)

GARDENING NOTEBOOK

1. Write a description of the gardens you visit using any notes you made in rough while you were there. Mount any postcards or pictures that you were able to get.
2. If you pass grazing animals on the way into the parks and gardens make notes on the various species of cattle and deer. Look at the way in which they keep the grass low and also eat the leaves and lower twigs on the branches of trees. Cattle, sheep, deer, and ponies and horses trim tree boughs close enough to the ground for them to reach, neatly making what is called the 'browse line'. Look out for this and try to draw the shape of some of the trees, in silhouette, once they have been trimmed in this way.
3. Look out for examples of topiary. Draw some of those you see, in the form of silhouettes.
4. Some of the gardens you go to may once have had famous owners or tenants. Try to find out whether they were statesmen, writers, artists or eminent in some other way and add such points of interest to the description of the garden after you have seen it.
5. On the way to see gardens look out for new landscaping of motorways or big road banks and roundabouts. Also look at the different layout and uses of all kinds of plants from annuals to trees, in gardens round such buildings as factories, tower blocks and schools. Write for information about these that you could include in this notebook to the planning department at the local government offices.

FURTHER TOPICS FOR DISCUSSION, OBSERVATION AND RESEARCH

1. Some of the gardens that you have visited may have included ornamental vegetables, such as beet with extra-dark leaves and members of the cabbage tribe with purple or frilled edges to the leaves, among their flower beds. Look out for more of these, such as sea-kale which has huge leaves and great clusters of honey-scented flowers.
2. Make notes on any information you can find in library books about the history of gardens and try to find out more about famous garden designers and landscapers. Sylvia Crowe is a famous modern garden-landscape architect whose work can be seen in many places, and Gertrude Jekyll was one of the first women, early this century, to become very well known by the designs and layouts she prepared for gardens.
3. Draw out some patterns and colour them for making flat 'carpet beds'. These were often used on parterres so that people could look down on them from the windows of their houses. Try to work out which tiny but colourful plants could be used to carry out your patterns.

11 · Indoor gardening

The rapidly increasing popularity of indoor gardening is now enabling everyone, even those who have no outdoor gardens, to indulge in the fascination of watching plant growth and development. Town schools can turn classrooms into living laboratories and the children can thereby study practical botany at first hand. This is a good introduction also to the delights of gardening and children may benefit from understanding simple scientific phenomena 'from the grass roots' for the rest of their lives. There is no doubt whatsoever that growing plants brighten rooms at home and in schools and make them more attractive places in which to live and work. Indoor plants also allow sick and housebound children and adults to participate in gardening activities (see Chapter 12).

Growing indoors gives an opportunity to watch undisturbed the development of plants, with the additional benefit of being able to handle and grow them in sheltered conditions during all seasons and weathers, even when rain is pouring down outside. This gives children, especially, a continuity of occupation and a chance of unbroken, interesting work that would be frequently interrupted or delayed while waiting for better weather in the garden.

There are plenty of occasions when indoor gardening with very young children proves to be even better than more distracting outdoor efforts. For example, such a simple starter as grass seed being carefully sprinkled on the bare soil in pots of growing bulbs can create interest. Keeping the cut-off tops of carrots, turnips, parsnips or beet which are being prepared for cooking, and putting them, cut side down, in a shallow saucer of water, so that new leaves start growing, also gives rise to questions and observations.

Pineapple tops, if treated in the same way, will provide a crown of young, interestingly shaped leaves. Although none of these leaf crowns can be expected to last long without roots, children enjoy watching their growth and they often trigger off an initial sense of enquiry into the growth and propagation of other plants. The growing of edible sprouting seeds will provide similar interest and this is discussed on p. 141.

PIPS, STONES AND SEEDS

Once children become interested in plants there are plenty which they can grow indoors. They will be most interested in growing new plants which they can see develop rather than in buying ready-grown ones.

If the pips, stones or pits from all kinds of ripe, fresh fruit, both home grown and foreign, are saved, washed and planted, some of them will produce an interesting variety of young plants and may even develop into mature fruit bearing plants if planted in greenhouses or sheltered gardens.

Children can try the seeds from the outside of strawberries and the inside of gooseberries and raspberries as well as the tougher apple and pear pips and the really hard plum or cherry stones. Others, from oranges, lemons, grapefruit, grapes, peaches and apricots, can also be sown. Some of the very hard fruit seeds may start growing faster if they are soaked for a couple of days before being planted. Date pits need a warm place in which to stand, in their pots of sand or seed-sowing compost. They produce strange-looking shoots with one grass-like leaf blade to begin with. This is replaced by subsequent leaves which are more palm-like, and good house plants can be grown from them for presents.

Pip-growing, either by individuals or groups of children, can be made into an interesting project. Each different kind of seed should be planted in a separate pot and labelled with its name, the number of seeds sown and the date. A group of children could plant, for example, the seed remains from a raw fruit pudding and then watch to see which of the various kinds come up first, the numbers and percentages of the total originally sown that germinated and, finally, which grow into the most successful plants.

Some of these seeds are slower to germinate than others but the soil in which they were planted must be kept damp all the time as roots may have started to grow even if nothing is visible from the top. Once a pot of soil dries out, the seed will die. Peanuts, amongst other kinds of unroasted nuts that could be tried, can be slow to start. Children should be warned that this may be the case but that it is worth waiting as the young plants, when they do begin to show, are attractive and unusual.

Obviously other planting and tending activities must go on all the time as well or interest may be lost, and it is sometimes up to the adult to remind young gardeners to look at their fruit seeds to see if anything is happening.

Seeds from other foreign plants, grown here as house plants, are also interesting to try. Some of them are available from seedsmen (see p. 165) and gardening shops and there are plenty to choose from. The instructions on the seed packets should be read carefully and the seeds must be given the right conditions for germination (see p. 49). Amongst the most rewarding seeds to try are:

bead berry plant (*Nertera granadensis*); cacti; castor oil plant (*Ricinis communis*); Christmas cherry (*Solanum* spp); flame nettle (*Coleus blumei*); also some succulent species.

PROPAGATION

As already discussed in Chapter 4, many plants can be grown from cuttings which are taken from healthy, strongly growing plants. Softwood or nodal cuttings can be used for geraniums (*Pelargonium* spp), busy Lizzies (*Impatiens* spp), *Tradescantia* spp and *Fuchsia* spp. Tradescantias are particularly good for beginners to try as they root very easily. When short whole shoots are pulled carefully from the plant just above the roots or cut as low as possible, they usually root very easily if potted up in

28. Leaves of two viviparous plants

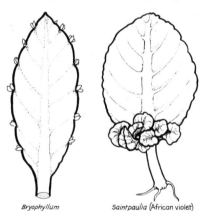

Bryophyllum   Saintpaulia (African violet)

growing compost. These basal-shoot cuttings can be tried with such plants as the trailing bellflower (*Campanula isophylla*), pansies and violas (*Viola* spp) and butterfly flowers (*Schizanthus* spp).

Leaf cuttings are an easy means of propagating some plants (see also p. 57). The whole leaf can be laid on the soil surface and the veins cut, with subjects like cape primroses (*Streptocarpus* hybrids) and *Begonia rex*, while the leaves of mother-in-law's tongue (*Sanseveria trifasciata*) should be chopped into short lengths and stuck into compost.

Viviparous plants produce plantlets on their leaves òr on special shoots or stolons. Some need a little encouragement in the way of careful cultivation before they produce young plants out of their living tissue but many do not.

The striped spider plant (*Chlorophytum comosum variegatum*) and mother of thousands (*Saxifraga stolonifera*) grow their young plants at the tips of long, arching shoots and the rosary vine (*Ceropegia woodii*) develops special aerial tubers from which the young plants grow. The succulent bryophyllums have rows of plantlets growing round the edge of their leaves, the New Zealand spleenwort (*Asplenium bulbiferum*) produces new plantlets on its fronds and the piggy-back plant (*Tolmeia menziesii*) also produces plantlets at the base of the leaves.

Any of the plantlets from the viviparous plants can be carefully removed, using tweezers for really small ones, and potted up into separate little pots.

CHOOSING AND CARING FOR ORNAMENTAL HOUSE PLANTS

There are an enormous number of ornamental house plants for sale and these, if they are carefully chosen, can really beautify rooms at home and in schools. The term 'house plant' covers both those that are grown for their attractive foliage and those that produce brightly coloured, showy flowers. Young people should consider all the places, such as entrance halls, living rooms, bedrooms, kitchens, corridors and bathrooms, which could be improved by having decorative plants growing in them. Before choosing plants for them they should obtain a room thermometer and make a note of the temperature there, regularly finding out if it remains constant or varies through the day. If pot plants are going to be grown in rooms where the temperature is likely to vary a lot, only the hardiest should be tried. The child should also see how much light reaches these places.

Most house plants are exotics, coming from warmer climates than our own, so it is important that the rules for keeping them healthy be learnt before buying and starting to grow or look after any of them. Ideally all house plants should have a level temperature of about 16 °C (60 °F) or at least one that never falls below 10 °C (50 °F). Frost is a killer for these tender plants and draughts are nearly as lethal.

Many indoor plants grow best in a moist, steamy atmosphere. They usually flourish in humid kitchens and bathrooms, as long as the temperature stays the same, day and night. In drier rooms, conditions can be improved for them by spraying or sponging the leaves daily. The upper and lower surfaces of all their leaves should be kept free of dust, and the appearance of glossy-leaved plants is improved if a sponging mixture of half milk and half water is sometimes used. It is also a good idea to stand such plants in a trough of moist peat which comes up to the rim of the pots.

The plants which like a humid atmosphere include African violets (*Saintpaulia* spp), which should never be watered from the top, and the delightful maidenhair ferns (*Adiantum* spp) which are not easy to grow successfully in a dry atmosphere.

Places in which house plants can be grown fall into three basic categories:

1. IN SOUTH FACING POSITIONS WHICH RECEIVE LONG PERIODS OF SUNSHINE EACH DAY Windowsills, ledges and table tops that get very hot sun for long periods in summer can only really be used for cacti and succulents. These are both groups that live naturally in great heat and drought and so are able to store water, when they get it, for use in dry periods.

Cacti store water in their stems and roots and only a few have proper leaves. Their strange, swollen stems are frequently protected with sharp spines, which prevent animals from browsing on them and demolishing them. These spines are actually modified leaves and, if they are examined carefully through a hand lens, it can be seen that they grow from tufts of short hairs, or from fluffier 'wool'. These tufts are called areoles. Particularly spiny cacti should be avoided with young children. Other succulent plants have no spines and store water in their thick leaves as well as in stems and roots. Some succulents which young people may like to grow are:

bowstring hemp (*Sanseveria sarmentosa laurentii*); houseleeks (*Sempervivum* spp); partridge breasted aloe (*Aloe variegata*).

If children are considering starting a collection of these plants they should go to a specialist grower (see p. 165). Some cactus nurseries have a selection of special plants for beginners, that are easy to look after. These usually include the Christmas cactus (*Zygocactus truncatus*) which produces brilliant crimson flowers at Christmas time. It is easy to grow and can be propagated from separate stem segments, by breaking them off one at a time and inserting them in potting compost.

2. IN A GOOD LIGHT, WITH SOME SUNLIGHT DAILY For windowsills and other places that have part sunlight and part shade during the day there is a greater choice of plants. This is a good position for the plants with variegated leaves as they need more light than many of the all-green leaved plants. A wide selection of plants can be grown under these

conditions and the following are some easier ones that children may like to try:

aluminium plant (*Pilea cadieri*); busy lizzie (*Impatiens sultani*); cheese plant (*Monstera deliciosa*); scented-leaf geraniums (*Pelargonium crispum*, lemon scented, and *P. tomentosum*, peppermint scented); Indian fig plant or rubber plant (*Ficus elastica decora*); mother-in-law's tongue (*Sanseveria trifasciata*); striped spider plant (*Chlorophytum comosum variegatum*); umbrella plant (*Cyperus alternifolia*).

3. IN SHADIER CONDITIONS WITH LITTLE OR NO SUNLIGHT   There are a few climbing plants with large green leaves, like the grape ivy (*Rhoicissus rhomboidea*) and the kangaroo ivy (*Cissus antarctica*), as well as many forms of true ornamental ivies (*Hedera* spp), that will grow well even towards the middle of an ordinarily light room. These are the plants to use to make living-plant room dividers or indoor screens. Various ferns can also be grown in such a situation, including bird's nest fern (*Asplenium nidus*), hartstongue fern (*Phyllitis scolopendrium*) and stag's horn fern (*Platycerium bifurcatum*). Other plants suitable for shady locations are the dragon plant (*Dracaena draco*) with all-green leaves, the oriental creeper (*Ampelopsis orientalis*) and the royal begonia (*Begonia rex*). The warmer the room the more light this last plant needs so it is best used in cool rooms in the shade.

Watering

Professional house-plant growers say that it is easier to kill a house plant by overwatering it than in any other way. This makes the compost waterlogged, forcing the air out and damaging the roots. The results of this soon show up by the withering and yellowing of the leaves. The surface of the compost should be dry to the touch before watering. It is important not to give many, small sprinklings but one thorough soaking instead, allowing surplus water to drain off, the plant should then be left alone until the surface is dry again. However, it is also important not to let the compost dry out completely. Peat-based potting composts dry quickly and are difficult to moisten again. So, the surface of the pot should be felt each day and the plant watered, above or below, when necessary—even in well-heated houses most plants will usually only need to be watered once a week, or twice at the most. Some plants like the large-flowered cultivated cyclamen and cape primroses (*Streptocarpus* hybrids) are better when watered from the bottom and do well if their pots are stood on trays of gravel and water.

If plants grown in schools have to be left during holidays, when there is no one to water them, their pots should be stood either in deep troughs of well-soaked peat or in water-covered gravel. They should be kept away from full sun. A simple system of gentle individual pot-watering can be made by grouping the pots as close together as possible, standing a bucket full of water on a lower level and leading a length of absorbent yarn out of the bucket and up to the soil of each pot. The yarn should be weighted so that it reaches the bottom of the bucket and will allow water to travel up it to the soil in the pot. Other, more costly pot-waterers can be obtained from florists, pot-plant nurseries and garden centres.

The older type clay flower pots are porous and allow moisture to seep through but many modern containers are in non-porous plastic. Therefore plants growing in clay pots will need watering more often than those in plastic pots. Clay pots should have good drainage layers of bits of broken pot, or crocks, placed in the bottom, and all pots should have good drainage holes in the base.

Feeding

Pot plants need some feeding and this is especially necessary while they are producing new leaves, flowers or fruit. Constant watering is likely to wash soil nutrients through, so special indoor plant fertilisers, made from organic materials whenever possible, should be bought and used strictly according to the instructions. Warn children never to give their plants more feed than is recommended by the fertiliser manufacturer and never to assume that all a sick plant needs is feeding. There are many other things that could be wrong with it.

Unfortunately there are many delicate house plants on the market and it is important that unknown plants are bought from a reliable source. It is best not to buy plants that have stood outside the shop in cold weather as they will probably die when brought back into the higher temperatures of the home. Some growers label their pot plants with coloured labels according to how easy they are to grow and whether they need any special conditions. But even so, difficulties in cultivation can, and do, arise. The following are some of the more common problems but, if in doubt, a good house-plant book or, if possible, the retailer from whom the plant was bought, can be consulted.

1. YELLOWING AND/OR DROOPING LEAVES
Suspect—incorrect watering (either too much or too little), cold, lack of light.
2. SHRIVELLING, DYING LEAVES
Suspect—incorrect watering, draughts, cold, too much sunshine.
3. LEAVES START FALLING OFF
Suspect—lack of light, incorrect watering, lack of humidity.

4. General sickliness

Suspect—incorrect room temperature, lack of humidity, draughts, incorrect watering.

Some pests, such as mites and caterpillars, may affect house plants and can sometimes be identified by the retailer. Plants can be sprayed with a non-poisonous solution (see p. 36) or the pests removed by hand or with tweezers.

Repotting

Some plants grow better in overcrowded conditions in pots that look far too small for them, so do not let children be in too much of a hurry to repot them unless the roots are really long and have started to grow out of the drainage holes, since the plant was bought. All indoor plants should be given a chance to get used to the conditions at home or school before they are potted-on. When it is really necessary, a good potting compost (see p. 42) should be used and repotting should be done in the spring when growth is most active and the fresh nutrients can be used. This allows the plant to settle down before the autumn and winter.

BULBS

Spring-flowering bulbs, grown in pots, bowls or small troughs, will give endless pleasure in the winter and will flower earlier than they do outside. Some have been prepared, or given a false winter, by putting them in refrigerators, so that they start growing directly they are planted. The favourites for indoor growing are hyacinths, some daffodils and narcissi, tulips, crocuses, dwarf irises and snowdrops.

All these bulbs can be grown in damp peat fibre or bulb fibre. This should be soaked and squeezed out before it is used. They can also be planted in soil, lightened with some sand or peat, or in a potting compost. The containers ought to have some drainage holes but, if there are none, pieces of charcoal can be added to the fibre, soil or compost (unless it already has some) to keep it sweet. The bulbs should not be completely covered, their tops should just be showing. Those not planted in squeezed-out fibre should then be watered.

To get the best blooms, the containers, once planted, should be kept in a dark, cool place so that the roots can grow well before the shoots start appearing. The containers should be examined from time to time to make sure that the fibre or other growing medium is kept damp. Cupboards in a school or house can be used, or an outdoor frame can be a good place for them and in this case the whole of the pot should be covered with

7·5–12·5 cm (3–5 in) of fine ash, which should be kept moist. Wherever the pots are kept should be mouse-proof, as mice enjoy eating some bulbs, especially tulips.

The bowls of bulbs should be kept in the dark for seven or eight weeks. The shoots may have begun to grow when they are taken out and will be pale and lacking in chlorophyll. The bowls should not be put in full light for a day or so, until the shoots are beginning to turn green. Once the flowers are over, the bulbs can be planted out in the garden, allowing the leaves to die back naturally so that natural foods made by them go back into the bulb for next year. Some may not flower for a year or two but they should recover and bloom again in time.

Some of the bulbs that are suggested for indoor pot culture are:

Crocuses—Dutch hybrids in golden yellow, purple, white or purple striped.
Hyacinths (prepared)—'Carnegie' and 'L'Innocence' (white); 'Anne Marie', 'Lady Derby' and 'Pink Pearl' (pink); 'Jan Bos' (red); 'City of Haarlem' (yellow); 'Bismarck', 'Delft Blue' and 'Ostara' (blue). Also multiflora and Roman hybrids,
Dwarf iris—*Iris reticulata.*
Narcissi[1] (prepared)—NN. 'Grand Soleil D'Or' (yellow) and 'Paper White' (white). (These two need sheltered positions when planted out.)
Snowdrops—single and double European *Galanthus nivalis.*
Tulips (dwarf growing)—'Brilliant Star' (red); 'Charles' (scarlet and yellow); 'Christmas Gold' (yellow); 'Christmas Marvel' (cherry pink); 'Diana' (white).

Bulbs can also be grown in water (see p. 143).

INDOOR HANGING BASKETS

If there is very little space for plants on sills or shelves, a pleasing indoor plant garden can be made in a hanging basket. This can hang from a hook in the ceiling, near the window, and could be fixed to a wall pulley so that it can be lowered for watering, though this is not essential, as long as the basket is within reach from steps. All kinds of plants can be used for an indoor hanging basket but here are some suggestions of particularly suitable trailing ones:

bellflower (*Campanula isophylla*); pendulous begonias (*Begonia* spp); *Columnea gloriosa*; creeping fig (*Ficus pumila*); *Fuchsia* spp; ivy-leaved

---

[1] The genus *Narcissus* includes the daffodils.

geranium (*Pelargonium hederifolium*); lobelia (*Lobelia pendula* 'Blue Cascade'); mother of thousands (*Saxifraga stolonifera*); ornamental ivies (*Hedera helix* and *canariensis* cultivars); sweetheart plant (*Philodendron scandens*); rat-tail cactus (*Aporocactus flagelliformis*); rosary vine (*Ceropegia woodii*); string of beads cactus (*Senecio rowleyanus*); *Tradescantia* spp; *Zebrina* spp.

All these plants will appreciate extra feeding in the form of organic fertiliser, and a light, mossy peat compost should be used or the loam-based John Innes No 2 or 3 would be suitable (see p. 42). Some form of drip tray under the basket, or a polythene liner, is necessary for indoor use. Plant-container slings can be fun to make using macramé (see p. 163) or other techniques in a range of materials including sisal, string and nylon threads.

A BOTTLE GARDEN

Some plants will grow very well inside large, corked bottles such as sweet jars, quart-holding Winchesters or large carboys. The bottle must be clean and dry inside and a bottom layer about 2·5 cm (1 in) of small gravel should be covered with 5 cm (2 in) of potting compost. This should be pressed down firmly with a tamper made from a cotton reel on a stick. Then, using a pair of long-handled wooden tongs, hollows can be scraped in the surface for the plants. The young plants should be lowered in gently with the tongs,

29. *Planting up a bottle garden*

spreading the roots as much as possible, before pushing compost over them. The compost should then be carefully firmed down all round the plants. Once the surface of the compost is firm it can be watered gently, being careful not to overwater. The cork can then be put in the bottle and the garden can be left in a warm, light place out of direct sunlight and should be disturbed as little as possible.

It is a good idea to use only a few plants at the beginning as most of them flourish and spread fast. Unrooted cuttings should not be put into the bottle garden in case they do not take and have to be removed. Plants should be chosen to give a range of leaf shapes and colours. This is a selection of those that usually do well in bottle gardens:

artillery plant (*Pilea muscosa*); aluminium plant (*Pilea cadieri*); creeping fig (*Ficus pumila*); ladder fern (*Nephrolepsis readii*); mother of thousands (*Saxi-*

fraga stolonifera); ornamental ivies (*Hedera* spp); pepper elder (*Peperomia scandens*); south sea laurel or croton (*Codiaeum variegatum pictum*); spider plant (*Chlorophytum comosum variegatum*); spiderwort (*Tradescantia albiflora tricolour*).

A MINIATURE FERNERY

Wild ferns grow in shady, damp places. These conditions can be reproduced in a very small way in a clear polythene box, as long as it has a close fitting lid. The box should be prepared by filling it with dampened peaty compost and putting the lid on before going into the countryside to look for some ferns. *Never dig up the ferns.* Look out for old fronds which usually have ripe spores on their undersides and shake them over the open box. Individual fern spores are often so tiny as to be virtually invisible. Once home the box should be kept in a shady part of a warm room and remain unopened. Ferns, unlike seed-producing plants, develop from spores and go through an extra stage in their development, which makes them even more interesting to study. The spores produce small, green, flat fern-like prothalli (singular—prothallus) on top of the soil and from these the tiny new ferns will eventually grow.

GROWING IN WATER

Growing plants temporarily in water provides a simple, exciting way to interest children in the whole question of root and shoot development. It *is* only a temporary way, unless plant nutrients are added (see hydroponics on p. 145), as tap or rainwater cannot provide all the complexity of trace elements that are necessary for continued growth. However, it is possible to demonstrate the basic way in which plants grow, often more easily than growing initially in soil. When subjects like the edible seed sprouters are grown, the process of root and shoot growth is very easy to see.

Edible sprouting seeds

These give an exciting and speedy way to produce salad plants indoors all the year through. They are simple to grow and can be eaten soon after they have sprouted, or produced their first young roots or shoots.

The seeds can be bought from seedsmen or health-food shops and should be stored in a cool, dry place until used. They only need water to start germinating, relying on the food supply in the seed embryo (see p. 49) for the necessary nutrients. The way to grow the best-known types is

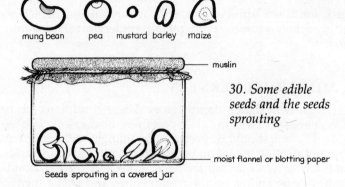

30. *Some edible
seeds and the seeds
sprouting*

Seeds sprouting in a covered jar

shown below but they should all be watched carefully to make sure that
they are kept moist and harvested when ready for eating. The time these
various seeds take to germinate depends a great deal on the temperature—they will grow faster in a warm room.

SEED	PLANTING	HARVESTING
Mustard, cress (sow two to three days before mustard if to be eaten together)	Sprinkle seeds on moistened flannel, blotting paper or clean sawdust in a saucer or flat dish and keep moist.	Cut off the growing shoots from the time they are 2·5 cm (1 in) long until they begin developing the first true leaves.
Alfalfa, fenugreek	Sprinkle seeds on moistened flannel, blotting paper or clean sawdust in a saucer or flat dish and keep moist.	Wash and eat whole as soon as the first roots and shoots appear. Will become tough if left too long.
Sunflower, marrow	Soak seed in water for 24 hours. Then sow in deeper dishes or pans with 2·5 cm (1 in) clean, damp sand at the bottom. Keep sand damp.	Wash to get rid of the hard seed covers then eat the rest of the sprouter from the time the shoot is 2·5 cm (1 in) until it gets too tough or first true leaves appear.
Maize, rye, triticale, oats, wheat	Soak in water for 24 hours. Then sow seeds in deeper dishes or pans with 2·5 cm (1 in) of clean, damp sand at the bottom. Keep sand damp.	Eat the green shoots once they are big enough to grasp until about 10 cm (4 in) tall. These shoots may need chopping finely before eating as they can be tough.

SEED	PLANTING	HARVESTING
Mung beans, soya beans, adzuki beans, chick peas, lentils	Soak in water for 24 hours and then put in clean jars with muslin coverings. Rinse the seeds with warm water twice a day, straining the water off through the muslin.	Eat whole from the time the roots are just over 1 cm (½ in) until they are 5–7·5 cm (2–3 in) long, when shoots will also have begun to grow.

Several seedsmen now sell seeds specially packed for sprouting and these can all be sprouted in a jam jar. It is best to eat sprouting seeds raw, as cooking, particularly in water, destroys some of their vitamin content. However, some of them, especially the beans and peas, can be fried quickly in oil and are both delicious and nutritious. Some shops, particularly those selling health foods, stock special containers in which several different batches of seeds can be sprouted simultaneously.

Bulbs

It is possible to grow bulbs in water alone because they use the food reserve that is stored in the swollen bases of last year's leaves to produce new leaves and flowers. However, they will have used up their food supply after growing only in water and will need to be planted out in the garden as soon as the flowers are over. This will give them a chance to recover but, even so, they will not produce flowers again for a year or two. When growing in water they should be started in the dark in the same way as soil-grown bulbs (see p. 138).

The choice of bulbs for growing successfully in water is really restricted to two or three kinds. These are hyacinths, bunch-flowered narcissi or jonquils, and scillas. Hyacinths do well in shaped glasses which hold the

31. Growing bulbs in water

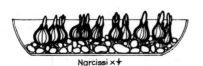

Narcissi × ⅓   Hyacinth × ⅓

bulbs so that they are just above the water. It is essential that the bulbs' bases are kept damp at first, with the water only just touching them. Then, when the roots appear, the water level should be a little lower. At this stage the water should not touch the bottom of the bulb, or it may rot it, but the roots must be able to reach into it.

A few cultivars of the bunch-flowered narcissi are especially good in water only. These should be planted in bowls containing washed gravel or pebbles, and water. Again, the bulbs' bases should only touch the water until the roots have started to grow and then the level should be lowered. The pebbles are needed to give the roots and growing shoots support and to anchor them as they get longer and taller.

The best kinds are *Narcissus* 'Cragford', with flat orange cups in the centre of creamy flowers, the all-gold 'Soleil D'Or' and the all-white 'Paper White' (see p. 139 for planting-out situations for the last two). These all have very fragrant flowers and are obtainable from stores, nurseries or straight from bulb growers. They should be planted as quickly as possible after purchase and, if specially prepared, will only take about five to seven weeks before coming into flower in a warm room.

Scillas can be grown in the same way as the bunch-flowered narcissi, but they take longer to come into flower as these bulbs are not usually specially prepared for early flowering.

Other plants

Acorns can often be found under oak trees in the autumn and may already have started to sprout a root. They can be grown-on, perched on top of a narrow-necked bottle of water, by keeping the root tip moist. Occasionally specially shaped glass containers, like miniature hyacinth glasses, are obtainable from florists. Acorns started off indoors through the winter can be planted out in the following spring to grow into sapling oak trees.

The stones of the avocado pear can also be germinated in water. The stone should be cleaned carefully to remove all flesh and then put, thicker end downwards, into a wide-necked bottle or jar, making sure that until the root begins growing the lower surface is kept damp. If there is not a bottle or jar available to fit it, the stone can be supported over the water by toothpicks, pricked in carefully a little way, round the sides. When the root grows well down into the water, the seedling can be planted out into a pot of soil or growing compost and it will grow into a glossy-leaved decorative house plant.

Many soft nodal cuttings (see p. 56) can be rooted in water. An African violet (*Saintpaulia*) leaf, complete with stem, or cuttings from tradescantias, for example, can be placed in bottles of water and the roots will grow. Others such as geraniums, can be put in a puddle pot—a pot of pebbles and water. All of these will need to be potted-up in growing compost once the roots are 2·5–5 cm (1–2 in) long.

There are many plants that can be grown in water throughout their lives as long as essential nutrients are added to the water. This technique, known as hydroponics, is used by some growers to produce vegetable crops, such as tomatoes and lettuce, as well as flower crops like chrysanthemums and carnations.

Commercially this is done in two ways. The newer Nutrient Film Technique involves supporting the plants on long trays through which a very thin film of nutrient solution is passed. This allows the roots to absorb the food they need but the formulation of the nutrient solution has to be rigidly monitored. Kits are available for gardeners to use in their greenhouses but care is needed to ensure success. The other commercial method can more easily be copied at home. This involves growing the plants in pots containing pebbles, gravel or plastic chips. This is similar to the methods, explained earlier, used for growing hyacinths or rooted cuttings. The main difference, however, is that inorganic fertilisers have to be added to maintain the plant's growth. House plants growing in this way can now be obtained from good florists, stores and garden centres.

WATER GARDENING INDOORS

An indoor water garden could be planned in a glass tank or bowl in which some of the small aquatic plants, both those which root at the bottom and those which float, could be grown (see p. 106). Such a miniature indoor aquarium could provide a temporary home for a few frog or toad tadpoles in the spring. Any creatures, especially amphibians, are interesting to watch but once they have legs they must be transferred to outdoor ponds from which they can crawl.

GARDENING NOTEBOOK

1. Make sure your planting diary is up to date.
2. If you are growing some unusual plants, such as cacti, from seed try to make some dated drawings as the seedlings germinate and then grow-on. Some of them start life looking very different from the shapes they will be when they mature.
3. Start a collection of pictures of house plants with brightly coloured

flowers. Mount them and try to find out about their countries of origin and any history that may be attached to their discovery.

4. Make a list of comments about the seed sprouters and their taste. For example, alfalfa, or lucerne, tastes like young peas to some people and mustard seedlings, more than those of cress, are hot, tasting already of the actual substance that will later be gathered in commercial crops from the buds of the plant to be dried and used as mustard. This list, with dates of when you planted and harvested the sprouters, could take the place of an actual planting diary here.

5. Keep a record of any plants which you may try growing by hydroponic methods.

FURTHER TOPICS FOR DISCUSSION, OBSERVATION AND RESEARCH

1. Both cacti and succulents are most interesting families of plants. Try to find out more about the places where they grow and also either go to a big nursery which specialises in them or visit exhibits of these plants at flower or agricultural shows. You may be surprised at the sizes some of the exhibitors' prize old specimens reach. Make a big, composite picture of cacti, showing some of their shapes.

2. Scented geraniums are easy to grow and provide leaves that can be used in the making of pot-pourri, a mixture of fragrant, dried flower petals and leaves, as well as, in a few instances, for flavouring jellies. Look out for different varieties of them in nurseries and notice how the fragrance of the leaves varies.

3. Find out if there is a commercial hydroponic unit in your area and, if so, write for permission to visit it. Make notes on this for your Gardening Notebook.

4. Discuss your ideas about the use of organic (natural) fertilisers for living, growing plants, some of which we eat, as opposed to those made from inorganic (artificial) substances or from over-concentrated forms of selected natural mineral elements.

12 · Gardening for the housebound and handicapped

There is no end to the activities that can be planned for housebound young gardeners as long as the subjects are kept fresh and interesting. This, of course, depends to a certain extent on suggestions made by helpful adults, but it is also up to the initiative of the young themselves. All the activities described in Chapter 11 can be enjoyed by the housebound child, as can those that come in this chapter under the special heading of *Gardening in Bed*.

FLOWER ARRANGING AND HANDICRAFTS

Many people are fascinated by the art of arranging flowers, and children, particularly, often have a sense of design and a natural ability to make a minimum of cut flowers look beautiful in simple ways. Some encouragement in extending their knowledge of other usable and available plant materials, such as twigs, leaves and fallen, lichened bark, would also be a good idea. The National Association of Flower Arrangement Societies (see p. 166) are always ready to promote children's interest. Local branches may be prepared to organise visiting demonstrations for those who are housebound or, indeed, for schools and hospitals.

It is now possible to study the subject of flower arrangement seriously and to gain qualifications, such as the City and Guilds of London Institute certificates. It is also possible to take a Girl Guide badge in flower arranging. Another way of increasing their interest in the subject would be for children to enter local flower-arranging competitions.

Apart from using freshly cut flowers, housebound young people could also press or preserve some flowers in a desiccant material for use later on, or dry everlasting flowers and grasses (see Fig. 15). There are plenty of other projects linked with gardening and flowers which could interest them, such as making containers for flower arrangements from clay or empty plastic containers and pictures using dried flowers, or designing and making useful things such as aprons or kneelers, for themselves and for presents for other gardeners.

GARDENING IN BED

It is perfectly possible for any child who is, or indeed may become, interested in gardening to enjoy some handling, growing and propagating of plants even if they have to stay in bed. If the patient is only in bed for a short time, a tray can be used to work on. If the stay is likely to be longer, young gardeners can work happily on an overbed trolley. One of the gardening demonstrators at the garden for the disabled at Syon Park invented a bed-width, narrow trolley that could be useful for many of

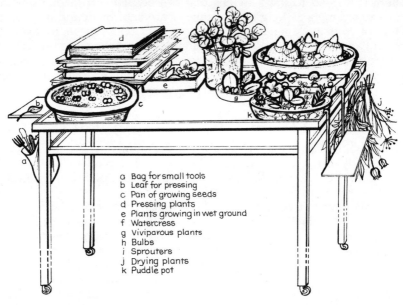

a Bag for small tools
b Leaf for pressing
c Pan of growing seeds
d Pressing plants
e Plants growing in wet ground
f Watercress
g Viviparous plants
h Bulbs
i Sprouters
j Drying plants
k Puddle pot

32. An overbed trolley

those who have to work in bed. He used it in a hospital in London where he went each week to teach children in the wards there. From it he showed various ideas on plant care and cultivation.

Trolleys like this are now on sale (addresses of manufacturers are available from the Disabled Living Foundation) but his original idea would not be too difficult for experienced do-it-yourself woodworkers to copy. The trolley must be on wheels and have a waterproofed top to the main shelf, but otherwise any simple form of movable, narrow table can be made, as long as its top clears the legs and bedclothes of the individual patient.

It is also important that the whole width of the top should be within easy, unstrained reach of its user. It is no good trying to fit in two under-shelves, nor making the trolley's width too extensive for the patient's easy arm movement. The diagram shows such an overbed trolley and some of the purposes for which it might be used. The top shelf can be used for the various plant-growing containers and other equipment. The two partial, bracketed or slide-under lower shelves can be used for scissors, kitchen knife, fork and spoons, a few simple tools, a bag of compost, seed packets and so on, and could also support screwed-in cup hooks on the outside from which dried and drying plant materials can be hung.

Plant-growing containers can be of all kinds, as long as they are fully waterproof and wide based. It is best to avoid using any tall water-holding vases, like hyacinth glasses, in case they are knocked over. Baby growing bags (see p. 91) are useful for cuttings but otherwise the choice of containers can be left to individual tastes.

Plants to grow

Apart from size, there are no restrictions on any types of indoor plants that young gardeners in bed could grow and any of the activities suggested in Chapter 11 could be tried. A puddle pot (shown in Fig. 32) using a fairly deep bowl with the bottom covered with small pebbles and holding about 2·5 cm (1 in) of water can be used to start off succulents and other cuttings.

Watercress is simple to grow in this way, providing the branches to be used, the pebbles and the bowl or puddle pot are all carefully washed first. Good, dark green, healthy-looking branches should be chosen and each carefully slipped under a pebble at the bottom of the pot so that it is anchored. The top of the original branches can be nipped or cut out and eaten when roots have formed on the underwater stem. The decapitated branch will then throw out new side branches which can in turn be carefully cut to eat. Freshening up the water in the pot can be carried out fairly frequently under a gently running tap, taking care not to disturb the watercress itself, and new pieces can be put in to replace any that look as if they will not grow any more.

Viviparous plants (see p. 133) make good parent plants from which successions of plantlets can be grown-on, and some forms of non-spiny cacti and succulents might be made into instant indoor miniature garden landscapes in pans. Small pieces of tufa rock (see p. 99) and mirrors to simulate pools could make these more interesting to plan. A miniature fernery and a bottle garden, as described in the previous chapter, are also both possibilities but these, being very slow growing, should not take up space on the trolley. A windowsill, or other light-available surface, would give additional space for the slower-growing plants.

All forms of miniature indoor gardens can be planned in bowls or, preferably, suitably deep-sided waterproof trays. Landscaping a tiny village (see p. 100), making a farm pond surrounded by model animals, with grass to be cut with scissors when it needs it, or a pond in a pleasure park surrounded by planted flower beds, are ideas that can be developed in many ways. The interest of boys could also be encouraged by the construction of a model roundabout or stretch of banked road on which model cars can be placed. The roundabout and banks can be made with heavily-pressed-down potting compost and then planted with grass seed and laid out 'beds' of miniature roses, dwarf conifers or flatter-growing plants. Even a rock garden with small pieces of rock could be made.

Anyone looking after children who are gardening in bed must keep an eye on their trolleys when they are not in use. The requirements of the plants growing in containers must be taken into consideration so that they are not left to dry out in hot, shaded rooms but are moved to situations where they get air and light.

Apart from visiting demonstrators, lecturers and others who could be invited to help to extend the interest of incapacitated gardeners, other visitors can also help. For example, bringing a bunch of watercress (from an accredited grower's stream) can be the start of a new project, as described above. Parents and friends should be on the lookout for interesting books about anything allied to plants. The lives of the plant hunters (see p. 161) often make exciting reading and the history of plants and their uses also increases awareness of the value of the plant world.

GARDENING FOR THE DISABLED

Many handicapped, even badly disabled, people who love flowers and are interested in growing plants are able to have the joy of gardening. There is no reason either why young people, in the same position, should not start gardening, even as complete beginners. Anyone, in fact, needing the support of a stick, calipers or a walking frame, who is unable to bend down to reach ground level, as well as those in wheelchairs, will find that there are now plenty of helpful aids. The therapeutic value of being able to take part in any plant-growing activities and of being associated with all facets of the plant world and the continual seasonal changes cannot be over estimated. Also, the production of changing, living plants, some with beautiful flowers, others which are edible, and therefore of benefit to friends and family, gives everybody a sense of companionship and of being part of a community.

A study of the subject of gardening for the disabled was started in 1964 by the Disabled Living Activities Group of the Central Council for the Disabled. When, in 1970, the Disabled Living Foundation (see p. 166) became registered as a separate charity, they took over the work of the original group.

Three study gardens were set up. One is attached to Mary Marlborough Lodge, the DLF research unit at the Nuffield Orthopaedic Centre, Oxford, where the head gardener, Mr Andrew White, has been doing wonderful pioneering work for many years, and where many patients work from wheelchairs. Then another was set up at Ingo Simon House, Mount Vernon Hospital, Northwood, Middlesex, where most of the patients suffer from rheumatic diseases. The third is at the Wolfson Rehabilitation Centre, Atkinson Morley Hospital, Wimbledon, Surrey. Studies on design for special gardens, on path surfaces, greenhouses, raised beds, lightweight, easily manoeuvrable and handy tools, among others, have been carried out there, also by Mr White and by patients, and the subject has now created a great deal of interest.

There are other demonstration gardens, including those at Syon Park Garden Centre, Brentford, Middlesex, at Capel Manor Institute of Horticulture, Waltham Cross, Hertfordshire and at the Royal Horticultural Society's gardens at Wisley, Surrey. Some interesting, private, raised-bed gardens are now on show and various authorities offer some provision for demonstrating and helping disabled people to carry on or begin gardening activities. To find out more about such schemes, enquiries should be made to occupational therapists. Disabled gardeners can also visit many other gardens open to the public (see p. 127) though it would be wise to check that wheelchairs can be accommodated first.

Another excellent charity, the Gardens for the Disabled Trust (see p. 166) helps to further the courage and energy of disabled people in encouraging them to make their lives fuller and more interesting by involving them in gardening activities. The Gardens for the Disabled Trust has two main functions – raising money in order to build, or help to build, special gardens for hospitals, residential and day centres, and running a garden club with the aim of linking disabled gardeners together, so that they may be encouraged and helped by each other's efforts. This club produces a lively newsletter which includes a children's page, and it offers advice on specially designed aids to easier gardening.

The only words of warning for disabled young people, and their parents and other adults, who are intending to embark on gardening are that they should first consult their doctors. Having obtained permission to go ahead, it is important to take it all easily and to have plenty of rests, but that is something which most gardeners should do anyhow.

There is no doubt that handling soil, and sorting out seeds, seedlings and light plant material of all kinds are helpful remedial activities. They benefit maladjusted children too, and teachers in day units all over the country are beginning to help children with difficulties to gain benefit, peace and calmness by introducing them to simple gardening activities. Teachers living in the London boroughs of Hillingdon, Brent, Richmond, Hounslow and Ealing may consult the Norwood Hall Institute of Horticultural and Agricultural Education (see p. 166). This is a wonderfully helpful institute which is ready to advise on gardening problems of all kinds. They also have an exceptionally interesting manual for blind gardeners.

Many of the activities suggested for able-bodied youngsters can also be enjoyed by the handicapped. Flowers, vegetables and fruit (see Chapters 5 and 6) can be grown, containers can be tended in the garden (see Chapter 7) and indoor plant activities (see Chapter 11) can be most rewarding as well.

A garden for the disabled

Perhaps the most important aspect when making a garden for the disabled is to consider the paths carefully. They must be level, have a non-slip surface and be wide enough to allow easy access for supports and walking frames, as well as having space for turning wheelchairs.

Raised beds or large outdoor containers with sides about 60 cm (2 ft) high filled with soil (see p. 91) are easier to work from than ground-level beds. If these are against walls they should not be more than 60 cm (2 ft) across but those with access all round can be double this. Special raised beds made of fibreglass can be obtained and also some raised containers of the same material. Other beds can be constructed with pre-cast concrete panels or paving slabs. It is also possible to build buttressed brick-sided beds and this might make a project for able-bodied children to carry out with a brick-building instructor. Raised beds must be set in below the level of the surrounding path although containers can stand on drainage props on the existing surface (see p. 91).

When planning a garden for the disabled the amount of space should first be surveyed and a plan made of how best to arrange the required raised beds and containers, remembering to allow for adequate path space. It is wise to lay paths in concrete, making certain that any paving slabs are safe, firm and level. The actual surface of the path or slabs should be slightly ridged, or ruffled, and then left to set hard.

When the paths are hardened, each bed can be dug out about 30 cm (1 ft) deep so that the upright side slabs can be squarely inserted. The bottom of each raised bed should be covered to at least 30 cm (1 ft) with hardcore or bits of broken bricks, medium-sized stones or some other undressed rubble. Some of the smaller material of this type should be kept for a 7·5–10 cm (3–4 in) cover over the top of this. Garden soil can then be used to fill the bed up to within 15 cm (6 in) of the top. For the topmost layer the best soil should be used. All raised beds and containers should be left for a week or more so that they can settle before planting.

The demonstration gardens give different ideas for planting various types of plants in separate beds and also some ways of landscaping others. Basically, though, these special beds can be used in the same way as other flower and vegetable plots at ground level, so that there is no need to stick to specific plants. The beds may be of a smaller area but the choice of what to grow is a question of individual ideas, and special favourites of all kinds can be tended.

There is, however, one extra requirement—that of hiding the ugly, rectangular corners and sides of these beds. This calls for careful cultivation of plants with pendulous, trailing stems. These can be chosen to match in to a certain extent with the other contents of the high plot using, for example, thymes (*Thymus serpyllum* 'Album' or 'Roseum') for beds of herbs or vegetables and brightly coloured ivy-leaved geraniums, lobelias and nasturtiums to enhance flower beds.

The demonstration garden at Syon Park has a small water garden in one of the raised beds which could be of much interest to young gardeners. The pond could be constructed in much the same way as described in Chapter 8 but in this case it would certainly be easier to buy an already-moulded lining. The water should attract similar insect visitors (see Chapter 8) even though the amphibians and hedgehogs might not be able to reach it. Aquatic plants of many different kinds, even some unusual ones like water chestnuts (*Trapa* spp), pickerel weed (*Pontederia cordata*) or miniature water lilies (*Nymphaea pygmaea* cultivars) could be tried, or even a collection of miniature floaters (see p. 106).

A booklet on a special garden for the disabled at Goodwood Park, West Sussex, is available from the Countryside Commission (see p. 166).

For information concerning Forestry Commission walks for the disabled see p. 166.

T o o l s   There are now plenty of specially designed, often lightweight or long-handled, tools of all kinds available for disabled gardeners, which will help partially to overcome many physical problems. It is important to get good initial advice about those which would be particularly suited to the needs of the individual gardener before becoming involved in unnecessary, perhaps even discouraging, difficulties or expense.

Both the Disabled Living Foundation and the Gardens for the Disabled

Trust will send descriptive leaflets and information about the special tools that are available for young gardeners. The latter even has a scheme whereby disabled gardeners may sometimes obtain small discounts from all kinds of suppliers, even from some of the plant and seed salesmen. Tools can sometimes be tried out at the various centres, but it is also sensible to ask the advice of personal doctors and physiotherapists as to tools which will suit individual gardener's capabilities.

WORK FOR YOUNG SIGHTLESS GARDENERS

As blind people often have an excellent and exceptional sense of hearing, this could be used very helpfully in gardens in a variety of ways. Children could learn to identify the different kinds of insects that visit flowers and bring about pollination, from the sounds they make as they fly. Initial teaching from expert entomologists would enable blind gardeners to learn to listen out for the differently pitched hummings and buzzings made by flower-visiting pollinators. Plenty is known about the importance of honey bees but much more information is required about helpful bumblebees and hover-flies.

Sightless gardeners interested in birds could help other people, including those with sight, to learn to recognise bird songs. Many public gardens, even in the heart of cities, have trees and shrubs that encourage birds to perch and sing from them. Excellent records of bird songs are obtainable from the Royal Society for the Protection of Birds (see p. 167) so the songs could be studied from these initially. Blind children who have become familiar with them could then share their knowledge with others.

Every young blind gardener should regard himself as an explorer, using senses of hearing and smell to increase the knowledge of other sightless people and helping those with sight to appreciate things that they may have missed before. The pleasures of flower scents, of touching plants, of learning to listen for infinitely small sounds can all be demonstrated and taught by blind gardeners. There are so many people whose knowledge of such things is still undeveloped that an enhancement of the pleasure to be derived from listening to the movement of leaves in the breeze, or determining a tree's identity by touching the bark, is badly needed.

Taped talks on gardening for the blind are available and further information is obtainable from the Royal National Institute for the Blind and also from the Disabled Living Foundation (see p. 166).

Gardens for the blind

Many towns and cities have gardens which have been planted with fragrant flowers and with plants and shrubs with leaves that are of varied textures especially for blind visitors to enjoy. Some of these have working areas for blind gardeners to use and gain ideas for working at home. Much experience of identifying plants by scent can be gained in these gardens, especially as some use braille labels for plant names. Other plants can be learnt by touch from the feel of the surface and outline of the leaves and the shape of the flowers. As blind people frequently have extremely sensitive fingertips, these experiences may be of far greater reward to them than to those who are able to see well.

Ways in which young blind people can use raised beds or ordinary level beds with concrete straight edges to act as guides, or work in narrow beds, can be discussed with other gardeners. Guiding planks or pliable curtain wires bent to varying shapes are the most basic aids, together, these days, with pelleted seeds which, when available, are so much easier to handle. Plants which will form the basis of an attractive scented garden include the aromatic herbs, roses (especially the thornless and the briars with the scented leaves), pinks (*Dianthus* spp) and a wide range of shrubs with scented flowers or leaves.

There is a walk suitable for blind people using a stick at Trent Park, Cockfosters, Barnet, Hertfordshire. This has braille labels, and a change of path surface indicates a point of interest. A leaflet which gives details and directions is available in braille from The Parks Manager, The Rookery, Trent Park, Cockfosters, Barnet, Hertfordshire. A scented garden for the blind is situated in Kew Gardens, Richmond, Surrey.

GARDENING NOTEBOOK

1. Keep a planting diary whenever possible, in the style suggested on p. 60.
2. Send for literature from the Disabled Living Foundation and from the Gardens for the Disabled Trust (see p. 166). Their pamphlets make good reading and contain useful information for your notebook.
3. Send for catalogues of plants that interest you especially and then read more about their cultivation and make notes for this book. Addresses can often be found in national papers on the same day as their gardening feature appears and in gardening magazines.

FURTHER TOPICS FOR DISCUSSION, OBSERVATION AND RESEARCH

1. Study the subject of flower scents and try to link them by association to already familiar smells, like lemon or pine. They can be roughly grouped like this but it is interesting to go more into the chemistry of flower scents and leaf aromas. There is a branch of little-known fringe-medicine, known as aromatherapy, which uses flower scents as curative, or at least ameliorative applications to the skin and it might be interesting to find out more about this. The address of the Aromatic Oil Company is given on p. 166.

2. Consider various forms of handwork linked with gardening and list possible future activities.

3. Investigate the possibility of contributing to an existing newsletter or taped 'magazine' for handicapped gardeners, or talk over the possibility of starting your own small club.

4. Ask adult friends to help explore the idea of growing plants for sale, using those that are simple to propagate and are popular but also of personal interest to you. Fascinating plants like poor man's orchids (*Pleione* spp) could be grown for sale as 'buttonhole' plants for special occasions. Older children especially should consider growing particular plants that have commercial possibilities, perhaps trying to make links with other young and, possibly, handicapped growers. Hobbies of this kind can be made to pay for themselves and might even lead to interesting careers.

Appendix 1 · Garden compost

Garden compost, made from various natural, organic materials described below, is a useful way of adding both humus and nutrients to the soil. Although peat and fertilisers could be used they would have to be bought, whereas garden compost can be made by rotting down garden and kitchen waste that would otherwise be entirely valueless.

A wide range of materials can be used to make compost:

1. Most green weeds before they seed—*except* couch grass or twitch (*Agropyron repens*), ground elder (*Aegopodium podagraria*), convolvulus or bindweed (*Calystegia sepium* and *Convolvulus arvensis*), lesser celandine (*Ranunculus ficaria*), slender speedwell (*Veronica filiformis*), giant hogweed (*Heracleum mantegazzianum*), creeping sorrel (*Rumex acetosella*), horsetails (*Equisetum* spp) and creeping buttercup (*Ranunculus repens*) (see Fig. 2). These should all go straight on to the bonfire because they are able to spread very rapidly, producing many new plants from bits of root, stem, leaf or tuber. Large plants of other weeds can be used chopped, before they seed, but do not use the woody stems which could take too long to rot down. Some common garden weeds are shown in Fig. 7.
2. Fresh mowings from lawns but not cut rough grass in seed.
3. A few bracken fronds (see p. 159), especially at the beginning of July.
4. Uncooked vegetable and fruit waste from the kitchen, chopped if large. Cooked leftover food should not be used as this makes the compost smell and attract flies.
5. Egg shells, tea leaves and coffee grounds.
6. Some torn-up newspaper.
7. Contents of vacuum cleaner bags as long as mats and carpets are *not* made from nylon or other artificial fibres.
8. Old rush mats, woollen clothes, etc, cut into small pieces, but *no* nylon, plastic (unless specifically labelled as biodegradable, that is made from materials which will rot down) or other artificial materials.
9. Swept up leaves can be added but actually are more valuable and rot down better into good leaf mould if they are piled into a separate heap.

The simplest way to make compost in the garden is in an uncovered heap which should be started straight on top of the soil. The soil bacteria which act in the rotting process need air, moisture and warmth in which to work and will get to work quicker if all the materials for composting are chopped up before being put on the heap.

Where the compost is made in a heap it is useful to have three fixed wooden, stiff wire mesh or concrete sides to enclose the heap, with the front open so that the heap can be turned at least once during the rotting-down process. A layer of soil, animal dung, bonemeal or 'shoddy' (wool waste) should be added after about every 20–23 cm (8–9 in) of plant or other material. It is also important to make at least one hole right down through the compost with a pointed stick to let the air in. The heap should be kept moist but not wet.

If a section of the compost heap is lifted up while it is rotting, it will be found that it is very warm and that 'fishing' or red worms are at work in it. In a few months, when the rotting-down process is complete and the compost is dark brown, crumbly and smells of good earth, the worms leave it to start work on other materials and help them decay. In most garden compost heaps these worms just appear from the earth underneath but a few can be bought from an angler's supply shop, if they are needed, and put into the bottom of a new compost heap.

If there is no room for a garden compost heap, it is perfectly possible to make good compost in a big, lidded can or bin which can stand in a garage, porch or patio, and if necessary special plastic containers can be bought at garden centres. The bottom of the bin should be covered with a 5 cm (2 in) layer of garden soil and then suitable composting materials can be put in as they become available. The lid should be kept on all the time, except when new materials are being added. When the bin is full, the rotting-down process can be speeded up if it is put in the sun, or a warm place, for several weeks.

Anyone without a garden can make good compost indoors for container and house plants from chopped up vegetable and household waste which is put into a tough, dark plastic bag. Again, 5 cm (2 in) of soil should be put in the bottom and then the other materials added. If there is not sufficient household material, fallen leaves from trees in streets or parks can be used. When full, this bag should be stored outside, if possible in the sun, to ripen, and the contents should be kept moist all the time, but not soaking wet.

Properly made compost does not attract flies and can be used in several ways to improve the garden soil. It can be spread on top of undug soil and turned in lightly as the ground is being dug. It can be used to spread on top of damp soil in summer as a mulch (which will be dug-in finally) to protect the soil from drying out and smother weed growth (see p. 43) and it can also be used as a top dressing around any special plants that need extra nourishment.

Appendix 2 · Poisonous plants

Many poisonous plants may be found in gardens, whether they are growing wild or are specially planted, and a list of the more common ones is included below. These are indicated in the index by the letter (**P**).

The intensity of their poisonous properties varies but all parts of the laburnum tree, including the seed-pods and seeds, are among the most dangerous. To hay-fever sufferers pollen from many different plants, not only grasses, is likely to start an attack and, to those with sensitive, fair skins, the juices from the broken stems of parsnip, giant hogweed, daffodils and many other plants are frequently to blame for causing rashes and blisters.

WILD PLANTS OR WEEDS   bracken (*Pteridium aquilinium*) but all right after composting; black and white bryony (*Tamus communis* and *Bryonia alba*); buttercups (*Ranunculus* spp); cuckoo pint or wild arum (*Arum maculatum*); henbane (*Hyoscyamus niger*); nightshades—black (*Solanum* mercury (*Mercurialis annua* and *perennis*); fool's parsley (*Aethusa cynapium*); giant hogweed (*Heracleum mantegazzianum*); hemlock (*Conium maculatum*); henbane (*Hyoscyanus niger*); nightshades—black (*Solanum nigrum*), green (*Solanum sarrachoides*), purple or bittersweet (*Solanum dulcamara*); old man's beard, wild clematis or travellers' joy (*Clematis vitalba*); poppies (*Papaver* spp); spurges (*Euphorbia* spp); stinking iris (*Iris foetidissima*); thorn apple (*Datura stramonium*).

CULTIVATED HERBACEOUS PLANTS   anemones (*Anemone* spp); autumn crocus (*Colchicum autumnale*); baneberry (*Actaea spicata*); bluebell (*Endymion nonscriptus*); brooms (*Cytisus* spp); Christmas rose (*Helleborus niger*); columbines (*Aquilegia* spp); daffodils and most narcissi (*Narcissus* spp); delphiniums (*Delphinium* spp); foxgloves (*Digitalis* spp); fritillary (*Fritillaria meleagris*); green hellebore or bearsfoot (*Helleborus viridis*); larkspur (*Delphinium ajacis*); lily-of-the-valley (*Convallaria majallis*); Lenten rose (*Helleborus orientalis*); monkshood (*Aconitum napellus*); poppies (*Papaver* spp); *Primula* spp; spurges (*Euphorbia* spp); winter aconite (*Eranthis hyemalis*).

SHRUBS AND TREES   alder buckthorn (*Rhamnus frangula*); box (*Buxus sempervirens*); buckthorn (*Rhamnus catharticus*); cherry laurel (*Prunus laurocerasus*); *Clematis* spp; *Daphne* spp; holly (*Ilex aquifolium*); laburnum or golden rain (*Laburnum anagyroides*); laurels (*Aucuba japonica* and cultivars);

mezereon (*Daphne mezereum*); mistletoe; privet (*Ligustrum ovalifolium*); spindle tree (*Euonymus europaeus*); spurge laurel (*Daphne laureola*); yews (*Taxus* spp); barberry (*Berberis* spp).

An excellent coloured chart showing clear pictures of some of the berried, poisonous plants, called *These Fruits are Dangerous*, is available from the Royal Society for the Prevention of Accidents (RoSPA) (see p. 167).

Booklist

WILDLIFE

NATURAL HISTORY
Natural History in the Garden, M. Chinery (Collins)
Wildlife Begins at Home, Tony Soper (Pan Books)

BIRDS
The Birds of Britain and Europe, Hermann Heinzel, Richard S. R. Fitter and John Parslow (Collins)
Feathers, Kathleen Shoesmith (Burke)

MAMMALS
Field Guide to Mammals, F. H. van den Brink (Collins)
The Observer's Book of Wild Animals, Maurice Burton (Warne)

REPTILES AND AMPHIBIANS
Field Guide to Reptiles and Amphibians, N. R. Arnold, J. A. Burton and D. W. Ovenden (Collins)

INSECTS
Field Guide to the Insects of Britain and Northern Europe, M. Chinery (Collins)
Butterflies, George Hyde, (Jarrold Colour Publications)
The Observer's Book of Butterflies, W. J. Stokoe (Warne)
Moths, George Hyde (Jarrold Colour Publications)
The Observer's Book of Larger Moths, R. L. E. Ford (Warne)
Plants and Beekeeping, F. N. Howes (Faber)
The World of a Beehive, John Powell (Faber)

POND LIFE
The Observer's Book of Pond Life, John Clegg (Warne)

MOLLUSCS (slugs and snails)
The Young Specialist Looks at Molluscs, Horst Janus (Burke)

WILD PLANTS

Wild Flowers of Britain and Northern Europe, Richard S. R. Fitter, Alistair Fitter and Marjorie Blamey (Collins)
The Observer's Book of Ferns, revised by Francis Rose (Warne)

Grasses, C. E. Hubbard (Penguin)
The Observer's Book of Grasses, Sedges and Rushes, Francis Rose (Warne)

GARDENING

The Dictionary of Garden Plants in Colour, Roy Hay and Patrick Synge (Ebury Press and Michael Joseph)
Collingridge Encyclopaedia of Gardening, edited by A. G. Hellyer (Collingridge)
Sanders Encyclopaedia of Gardening: A Dictionary of Plants, including their Cultivation and Propagation, edited by A. G. Hellyer (Hamlyn)

The *Wisley Handbooks* (Royal Horticultural Society) cover many groups of plants and gardening activities such as alpines without a rock garden, cacti, chrysanthemums, ferns, flower arranging, fruit growing, ground-cover plants, heaths and heathers, hedges and screens, herbaceous plants, ivies, plants for the shade, plants for small gardens, wall shrubs and climbers, and water gardens.

BULBS
A Guide to Bulbs, Patrick Synge (Collins)

FRUIT AND VEGETABLE GROWING
The Fruit Garden Displayed (Royal Horticultural Society)
Grow Your Own Fruit and Vegetables, Lawrence D. Hills (Faber)
Soft Fruit Growing, Raymond Bush (Penguin)
Tree Fruit Growing, Raymond Bush (Penguin)

GARDENING FOR THE DISABLED
Gardening for the Handicapped, Betty Massingham (Shire Publications)
Gardening for the Physically Handicapped and Elderly, Mary Chaplin (Batsford)

GROUND COVER PLANTS
Ground Cover Plants, Margery Fish (Faber)

HERBS
A Modern Herbal, M. Grieve (Penguin)
Herbs for First Aid and Minor Ailments, 'Ceres' (Thorsons)

HISTORY
History of Gardens, Christopher Thacker (Croom Helm)

HOUSE PLANTS
House Plants, Cacti and Succulents, W. Davidson and T. Rochford (Hamlyn)

ORGANIC GARDENING
Common-Sense Compost Making, M. E. Bruce (Faber)
Compost Gardening, W. Shewell-Cooper (David and Charles)
Down to Earth Gardening, Lawrence D. Hills (Faber)
Soil, Humus and Health, W. Shewell-Cooper (David and Charles)
Biological Pest Control Report No. 3 (Henry Doubleday Research Association)
Pest Control without Poisons (Henry Doubleday Research Association)
Fertility without Fertilisers (Henry Doubleday Research Association)

ROCK GARDENING
A Handbook of Rock Gardening, edited by Roy Elliott (Alpine Garden Society)

TREES AND SHRUBS

Field Guide to the Trees of Britain and Northern Europe, A. Mitchell (Collins)
Hillier's Manual of Trees and Shrubs, R. Lancaster (Hilliers)
Trees and Shrubs valuable to Bees, M. F. Mountain (International Bee Research Association)
Discovering Topiary, Margaret Baker (Shire Publications)

MACRAMÉ

Macramé in Easy Stages, B. Pegg (Studio Vista)
Macramé: A comprehensive guide, Heidy Willsmore (Faber)

WALL CHART AND FILM SUPPLIERS

British Museum; Forestry Commission (trees); Council for Nature; Guild of Sound and Vision (films); National Trust; Pictorial Charts Educational Trust (ecology); Royal Society for the Protection of Birds (birds); Frederick Warne Ltd, 40 Bedford Square, London, WC1B 3HE (butterflies).
Addresses are on p. 166.

Some useful addresses

PLANTS AND SEEDS

ALPINES AND ROCK PLANTS   Allenby's Nurseries, Elvington, York;
C. G. Hollett, Greenbank Nursery, Sedburgh, Yorkshire; Jack Drake,
Inshriach Nursery, Aviemore, Inverness-shire; W.E.Th. Ingwersen Ltd,
Birch Farm, Gravetye, East Grinstead, West Sussex (catalogue 25p);
Paradise Nurseries, Bradford, Yorkshire.

BULBS   Broadleigh Gardens, Bishops Hull, Taunton, Somerset
(catalogue 25p); Parkers, 452 Chester Road, Old Trafford, Manchester;
Van Tubergen, 5 Ranelagh Gardens, London SW6 3JY.

CACTI   Abbey Brook Cactus Nursery, Old Hackney Lane, Matlock,
Derbyshire; Craig House Nursery, Dundedin, Renacres Lane, Shirdley,
Halsall, Ormskirk, Lancashire; Holly Gate Nurseries, Billingshurst Lane,
Ashington, West Sussex.

FERNS   Fibrex Nurseries Ltd, Harvey Road, Evesham, Worcestershire;
Southdown Nurseries, Redruth, Cornwall.

PLANTS FOR DRYING   Elm House Nurseries, Walpole St Peter,
Wisbech, Cambridgeshire.

ROSES   Andersons, 12 Cults, Aberdeen, Scotland; C. Gregory and Son,
Nottingham.

SEEDS   Bees Ltd, Sealand, Chester; Saracen Truth Seeds, Challock,
Ashford, Kent; Suttons Seeds, Hele Road, Torquay, Devon; Thompson
and Morgan Ltd, Ipswich, Suffolk.

STRAWBERRIES AND CONTAINERS   Ken Muir, Honeypot Farm,
Weeley Heath, Clacton-on-Sea, Essex.

TREES, SHRUBS AND HERBACEOUS PLANTS   Highfield Nurseries,
Whitminster, Gloucestershire; Hilliers, Winchester, Hampshire; Sun-
ningdale Nurseries, Windlesham, Surrey.

WATER-GARDEN PLANTS   D. J. Case, Higher End Nursery, Hale,
Fordingbridge, Hampshire (catalogue 25p); Stapely Water Gardens,
Stapely, Nantwich, Cheshire; Wildwood Water Gardens Ltd, Theobalds
Park Road, Crews Hill, Enfield, Middlesex.

ORGANIC FERTILISERS

Maxicrop Ltd, London Road, Great Shelford, Cambridgeshire; Organic Concentrates Ltd, Chalfont St Giles, Buckinghamshire; Seaweed Ltd, Moycullen, Co Galway, Ireland.

ASSOCIATIONS, GOVERNMENT DEPARTMENTS, WALL CHART AND FILM SUPPLIERS, ETC

Alpine Garden Society, The Secretary, Lye End Link, St John's, Woking, Surrey.
Aromatic Oil Company, 12 Littlegate Street, Oxford.
British Museum Natural History Publications Department, Cromwell Road, London SW7 5BD.
Countryside Commission, 1 Cambridge Gate, Regents Park, London NW1 4JY.
Council for Environmental Conservation, 2 Greville Street, London EC1N 8AX.
Disabled Living Foundation, 346 Kensington High Street, London W14 6NS.
Forestry Commission, 231 Corstophine Road, Edinburgh EH12 7AT.
Gardens for the Disabled Trust, c/o Goddards Green House, Biddenden, Kent.
Good Gardening Association, Arkley Manor, Arkley, Barnet, Hertfordshire.
Guild of Sound and Vision, Woodston House, Oundle Road, Peterborough PE2 9PZ.
Henry Doubleday Association, Bocking, Braintree, Essex.
International Bee Research Association, Hill House, Gerrards Cross, Buckinghamshire.
Ministry of Agriculture, Fisheries and Food, 1 Whitehall Place, London SW1A 2HH.
National Association of Flower Arranging Societies (NAFAS), 21A Denbigh Place, London SW1V 2HF.
National Trust, 42 Queen Anne's Gate, London SW1H 9AH.
Nature Conservancy Council, 19 Belgrave Square, London SW1X 8PY.
Norwood Hall Institute of Horticulture and Agriculture, Norwood Green, Southall, Middlesex.
Pictorial Charts Educational Trust, 27 Kirchen Road, West Ealing, London W13 OUD.
Royal Horticultural Society, Vincent Square, London SW1P 2PE.
Royal National Institute for the Blind, 224 Great Portland Street, London W1N 6AA.

Royal Society for the Prevention of Accidents (RoSPA), Cannon House, The Priory, Queensway, Birmingham B4 6BS.

Royal Society for the Protection of Birds, The Lodge, Sandy, Bedfordshire.

The Wildflower Society (Junior Membership), Harvest House, Reading, Berkshire.

When writing to request information, lists, etc, a stamped, self-addressed envelope should always be sent.

General Index

NOTE: Botanical names of plants, including those such as *Anchusa*, *Chrysanthemum*, *Fuchsia*, *Phlox* and *Rhododendron* which have no separate common name, are in the Botanical Index of Genera, p. 174. Plants which have very similar botanical and common names, for example rose/*Rosa*, lily/*Lilium*, thyme/*Thymus* and tulip/*Tulipa*, are included in both indexes.

The symbol **(P)** indicates a poisonous plant

Botanical Index of Genera

See NOTE on p. 167

(P) indicates that some species (see p. 74) are poisonous